BLUE MOON VEGAN

OVER 100 PLANT-BASED, GLUTEN-FREE RECIPES FOR HEALTHY LIVING

BY PAULA MARIE COOMER
WITH JAN CALVERT

FOOD PHOTOGRAPHY BY SUZI HATHAWAY

Copyright 2015 Paula Marie Coomer

This work is licensed under a Creative Commons
Attribution-Noncommercial-No Derivative Works 3.0 Unported License.
Attribution — You must attribute the work in the manner specified by the author or licensor
(but not in any way that suggests that they endorse you or your use of the work).
Noncommercial — You may not use this work for commercial purposes.
No Derivative Works — You may not alter, transform, or build upon this work.

Inquiries about additional permissions
should be directed to: permissions@fawkespress.com

Cover Design by Greg Simanson

Interior design by Kate Burkett

Edited by Bethany Root

Trademarks and brands are the property of their respective owners. No claim is made to them and no endorsement of them by this book or recipes is implied or claimed.

ISBN 978-1-945419-14-0

ePub ISBN 978-1-945419-15-7

Library of Congress Control Number: 2015900828

For Marba Lou, Delta, Hazel, and, of course, Phil

CONTENTS

ACKNOWLEDGMENTS *7*

INTRODUCTION *11*

IN THE PANTRY *21*

SIPS AND SMOOTHIES *35*

GOOD MORNING *43*

SALADS AND SANDWICHES *53*

SOUP KETTLE *67*

ON THE SIDE *95*

CENTER STAGE *109*

FROM THE BAKERY *129*

YUMMIES AND PORTABLES *147*

WHERE TO BUY THINGS *155*

COOL, TRUSTWORTHY RESOURCES *157*

VEGAN AND GLUTEN-FREE PROTEIN SOURCES *159*

NOTE FROM PAULA MARIE COOMER *163*

INDEX *165*

ACKNOWLEDGMENTS

No book is written without a considerable amount of help, but in this case, *Blue Moon Vegan* never would have materialized had it not been for Kate Burkett, my book manager at Booktrope, whose subtle insistence and belief in its value finally convinced me to take on the project. Kate has been a phenomenal supporter of my food writing, and I feel very lucky to have her in my corner. Just yesterday a fellow author reminded me that during a radio interview earlier this year, I had sworn that I would not write a follow-up cookbook to my food memoir *Blue Moon Vegetarian*. Kate's faith in my abilities left me no choice but to take the leap. She keeps maneuvering me to the next level, and what was once a working relationship now is friendship. I no longer resist her quiet prodding.

From the beginning, my husband Phil and I doubted that we could come up with enough recipes to fill an entire cookbook. We have been living all this time convinced that *Blue Moon Vegetarian* was an accident and not repeatable. From all evidence, it appears we were wrong. Just this morning he came to me with an idea for a rice dish that features garlic scapes and dried cranberries steeped in vegetable stock. People for whom *haute cuisine* is not inherent don't wake up imagining new flavor intersections or unique dishes to create.

As for me, I keep saying, "I'm a poet. I'm a writer of fiction. I'm not a cook."

Yet here I am. A number of these recipes were created by Phil, and most of the baked goods were contributed by Jan Calvert, owner of Bridge Baking Company, the wondrous gluten-free bakery just across the river from us in Lewiston, Idaho. But the rest of them are mine, so I guess I do have to stand up and admit that I have my fair share of ability in the kitchen. It's my feminist nature that makes me want to fight it. In the end, as I've struggled to bring this book together, I've understood that creating with food is truly an art and not necessarily in competition with my married-but-not-domestic image of myself. Phil still spends more time cooking than I do, but if I am going to be in the kitchen, I much prefer to be inventing.

And I do know where this ability comes from. I spent many hours as a child observing and following around in the kitchens of their mountain homesteads my two grandmothers, both of whom could make magic arise from a collection of meager ingredients. They carried water from the well, cooked and baked on wood cook stoves, grew and harvested and canned and preserved almost everything that passed to their mouths from the table. I remain humbled by the knowledge those two women carried within themselves—the wisdom of plants, the ways of the natural world, the bounty that could be brought forth from well-nurtured soil. My wish is that by writing this cookbook, I have somehow cast back onto the world their love and nurturing, healing woman spirits. And that by doing so, I have laid a similar path for my own three granddaughter-miracles.

A book also does not happen without the gift of space, and for me that comes down to Dawn Abbott and the Blue Lantern Coffee House, also across the river in Lewiston. As any student of sociology knows, we humans require what is known as *third space*—a regular spot apart from home and job—where we can relax, be ourselves, and engage with others. For me that is Dawn's place. She has endured me for hours and hours and days and days in her backroom as I hovered over the keyboard and sipped her fine espresso, listened and mourned with me when, on the day of my original deadline, the entire manuscript for this book suddenly and irretrievably vanished from my hard drive. She has hosted my readings and a series of cooking classes; cajoled and advised; and provided a beautiful, soothing, yet dynamic setting filled with art, plant life, and antiques—a perfect backdrop for her baked goods made with organic and local ingredients, as well as her very fine fair trade coffee. She is a force of her own: the persistent traffic over her transom and the growing familiarity of those faces proves that she is providing a third space to many, indeed.

I'm not sure which came first: my panic over agreeing to do a follow-up to *Blue Moon Vegetarian*, or my frantic recognition of the fact that I had no idea what recipes would go in a breads and desserts section. I've gotten better at gluten-free baking, but I felt my best choice was to visit Jan Calvert, who owns our region's only gluten-free bakery and who also had hosted a *Blue Moon Vegetarian* event. Bless her heart. She is not vegan, but she had started to offer egg-free and dairy-free items on Saturdays as a result of customer requests. Without skipping a beat, she agreed to continue converting her bestsellers for inclusion in *Blue Moon Vegan*. Her only question was, "What's my limit on the number of recipes?" For readers who have tried and failed to bake tender breads and pastries using gluten-free ingredients, you are home free. Jan's method of weighing flours instead of measuring makes perfect sense to me and also explains why I used to get inconsistent results when baking with wheat flour. I have never been overly fond of cinnamon rolls—in fact, we eat very few sweet things at our house—but when she sat me down to test her vegan, gluten-free version, I almost cried. It tasted that wonderful. Soft and full-bodied, it did not leave me with a sugar buzz or the all-body wheat-sizzle I used to get after eating a pastry. In other words, I felt nourished. By a pastry! During the past few months, Jan also has become a dear friend, and once this book goes to editing, we have a celebration evening planned that we both fully intend to keep.I also must mention Mallory Fry and Kaitlyn Bergman. These two very beautiful young women design the most fabulous craft cocktails for one of our neighborhood gathering places, also using local ingredients in season and organically-grown when possible. I will have a price to pay when my mother reads this, since she raised me a teetotaler, but I felt these recipes were too yummy—even as virgin drinks—not to include. They are flat medicinal and are satisfying in a way that does not invite abuse. A small amount of alcohol now and again has health payoffs in the form of the socialization and relaxation that comes with enjoying them, not to mention benefits to the cardiovascular system, but I in no way advocate habitual use, and I believe we all need to very careful about the amount we do consume.

Once you open these pages and view the stunning food photography, you will understand why I fairly swooned the first time I saw the results of the photo shoot for the book. Suzi Hathaway operates as Suzi Hathaway Photography in Meridian, Idaho, and I know her for her portraiture. In fact, she was the photographer for my and Phil's wedding. Her eye for color and composition speaks for itself, but it's the simple, elegant arrangements that take my breath away. What she captures visually is the life of fresh ingredients and the vigor they contain, and her ability to do so amounts to the production of art. She did this all while being not only the mother of a seven- and four-year-old, but also five months pregnant and, on some days—rather ironically, we both thought—incapacitated by nausea.

Lastly, I am so in love with my publisher, Booktrope. Ken Shear and Katherine Fye Sears are trailblazers in the world of small presses, and their team of rowdies—Jesse James Freeman, Andy Roberts, Greg Simanson, Kate Burkett, my editor Bethany Root, and dozens of designers, proofreaders, and marketing people—are unparalleled in the publishing industry. I am proud and honored to be working with them on this fourth book and to be looking down the road at several more. If all goes right, next year they will be releasing *Blue Moon Medicine Woman*, as well as *Blue Moon Folkways in the Kitchen*, books I hope will capture and preserve the mountain wisdom and talents of my mother and grandmothers.

INTRODUCTION

The fact that I am quite fortunate is not lost on me. I do, after all, retain the same body parts afforded me at birth (minus a pair of tonsils and a gall bladder). I am educated, reasonably sane, and of moderate but sufficient means at least to make some decisions about myself and the way I live. Having been schooled as a nurse, I understand the relationship between food, health, and longevity. I understand that it is *up to me*, that I have the freedom and duty to make decisions that will benefit me and help me achieve whatever optimum state I am capable of—so that I might serve those I love as well as my fellow humans, even if only in some small way.

Not everyone is so lucky. By 2012 figures, forty-nine million people in the United States are at risk for going to sleep hungry tonight (see *Cool, Trustworthy Resources* on page 157). That is one out of every seven Americans. If you suggest to these people that they should embrace veganism or that processed food is making them sick, they will likely laugh in your face. Twenty-eight million will wonder not whether they should give up cream in their coffee, but whether they will have anything to eat tomorrow. Nearly sixteen million children aged eighteen years or younger will spend yet another day without access to the nutrients necessary to maintain health. If not corrected, 100 percent of them will eventually need medical attention for conditions stemming from inadequate nutrition. For children under five, that also translates to undeveloped brains, mental and behavioral issues, and impaired immune systems—all of which one day will require infusions of taxpayer dollars.

An additional 23.5 million working class people live in food deserts—urban and rural areas where fast food restaurants and convenience stores are the only sources of food available, with no produce stores, no groceries, no growers' markets. These people will suffer a different brand of hunger. The hunger bestowed by illusion, in this case brought about by high-calorie, low-cost foodstuffs that generate fullness without nutrients. Fool's gold. These people are at very high risk for obesity, early heart disease, diabetes, and a laundry list of other conditions starting with anemia and eczema and ending with osteoporosis and cancers.

For those of us who are financially able to make choices about what we eat, it is my opinion that we have an obligation to choose responsibly: to eat low on the food chain, to avoid foods that would make us ill, and to seek the good health that a diet of whole, fresh foods can provide. By extension, we can change the food situation in America by challenging our political system to support one of the most basic of human rights—easy, ready, and affordable access to quality, nutritious foods. As with all elemental human necessities such as water and energy, I believe no one should be allowed to make more than a modest living off the production of food.

WHY VEGAN?

My husband Phil and I chose to go vegan in 2012 after two years of vegetarianism and after viewing a film called *Forks over Knives*. (Read our story in *Blue Moon Vegetarian: Reflections, Recipes, and Advice for a Plant-Based Diet*, Booktrope, 2013.) This documentary made famous an expansive dietary study conducted in China in the 1980s (see *Cool, Trustworthy Resources* on page 157). Many thousands of Chinese peasants were interviewed and their blood analyzed in an effort to understand why, after the Western diet was introduced on that continent, people began to exhibit the same disease states and causes of death as westerners—cancer, diabetes, and heart disease—when they previously had been nearly non-existent.

What was discovered was that people who ate closest to a ninety-five percent plant-based diet—in other words, the poorest who relied mostly on what they grew themselves—had the lowest incidence of disease. In fact, they were afflicted by virtually none of the big monsters that regularly kill Americans. As a former registered nurse, I knew of this study but had not thought of it since my years as an undergraduate science major. But Phil had been taking an oral hypoglycemic for several years to control his blood sugar, and we were looking for a non-pharmaceutical solution—not a treatment, but a cure.

On the spot we made a decision to explore the vegan life, deciding first to give up dairy products. Seemingly overnight, a rather amazing array of health-related troubles fell away. We both had suffered for decades—me with earaches, Phil with sinus infections and allergies—and had taken a riot of antibiotics (I delve into the relationship between antibiotic use and yeast overgrowth in *Blue Moon Vegetarian*). Not to get too personal, but for each of us, it took ten days for our heads to stop draining.

Once we had recovered from dairy detox, we lost our taste for eggs and eventually let go of those, too—although I did for a while continue to use them in baking, simply because I didn't know what else to do.

Some folks choose the vegan path because they care too much about animals to eat them. We never thought about that part, since we had a habit of buying meat from local ranchers who put care into the creatures they reared and sold. Phil and I both cling to the idea that it is better to support our neighbors than big business. We'd like to see a return to commerce where the center of its life is the community. We'd much rather help our neighbor buy a new car or boat than add more pennies to the pot of already-wealthy folks heading up large corporations.

But I will tell you that the lives and treatment of pigs, cows, and chickens meant for wholesale slaughter are deplorable. If you knew the truth about it, you'd never sink your teeth into grocery-store animal flesh again. One film that has opened the eyes of many is *Food, Inc.*, and I highly recommend it, along with Deborah Koons Garcia's *Symphony of the Soil*.

At this point, as much as possible, we eat raw foods. We focus on vegetables—and a wide variety of them—and then nuts, seeds, nut butter, legumes, coconut yogurt and coconut milk, and on occasion, grains such as certified gluten-free oats, millet, and quinoa. Five days a week we each drink a Phil's Daily Hemp Shake (see page 35), which is made with fresh or frozen fruit, kale or spinach, and hemp protein powder—a ritual that has helped us lose weight, although Phil more so than I. We try to keep dark chocolate on hand, for the heart benefits it is known to lend, and eat an ounce each most nights, especially during fall and winter. We both take a Vitamin B12 supplement—vegans have almost no other way of getting it and deficiencies can cause terrible damage to the spine—and I take calcium because of worries we women have about the quality of our bone structure as we age. We both take Vitamin D3, which is necessary to facilitate calcium absorption and which the body normally manufactures itself in response to sun exposure. Since we live so far north and have indoor jobs, we need to ingest supplements in order to avoid deficiencies. Phil also drinks aloe vera juice every day, which for several years now has kept his diverticulosis quiet.

WHY GLUTEN-FREE?

Animal protein—along with a number of other foods, and, in particular, processed foods—creates an inflammatory state in the body, and chronic inflammation is the basis of most diseases. What happened to me, and what happens to many people, I've learned, is that once I got animal products out of my diet and my system began recovering, like the layers of an onion falling away, it became clear that I could not tolerate foods made with wheat, barley, rye, and spelt. When I consumed them, my face, arms, hands, and feet swelled, and I became lethargic.

It was my private secret: for as long as I can remember, I had struggled with fluctuating energy levels, mild dysthymia (vague melancholy), and sleep disturbances. In short, I could fall asleep on a dime in the middle of the day, but sometimes at night (and there was no predicting it) I could not sleep at all. I also had the worst immune system of just about anyone in history. Catching a cold translated to as much as two weeks away from work. The flu meant three weeks of mostly sofa time with several more weeks spent striving to rebuild myself. And PMS? You don't want to know. At times I have wondered whether I settled on an academic teaching job because it meant I could work primarily from home. No one knew I took a minimum of one nap a day. No one knew how many days I spent in my pajamas.

Finally, in 2012, rescue arrived. I was at the wake of my longtime friend Rachel, talking with her sister Jeanne, when a lovely little girl came bounding up with a chocolate cupcake decorated with a little twirl of frosting. "Can I have this, Mom?" she asked.

Even now I can feel my raised eyebrows—I knew that Jeanne had not recently borne any children.

"Only the very top of the frosting," Jeanne said.

Again with my raised eyebrows.

"Gluten-intolerant," she said. "We adopted her two years ago. Lethargic and developmentally delayed. Finally found the right doctor. Got gluten out of her diet and, well, you can see. We were feeding her barley cereal. Every kid starts out on barley cereal. I guess sometimes the only symptom of gluten intolerance is sleepiness."

And indeed I could see. The child was brilliantly beautiful, had the energy of a hummingbird, swallowed her little dollop of frosting and was off. "You mean celiac?" I asked. "She has celiac disease?"

"No, gluten intolerance. Two different things."

Meanwhile, I felt like I'd taken a bullet to the brain. *Sometimes the only symptom is sleepiness.*

Gluten intolerance. I certainly understood celiac disease, but this was new. In that flash of a nanosecond I glimpsed something I had not been able to interpret before—why I regularly lingered in front of the gluten-free section at the grocery store, wondering at the mystery of those products. Obviously, some part of me knew.

But, oh my, is denial a powerful thing. I could not bring myself to go to a doctor to get tested. I do not trust modern medicine. If you can't pay your bill, they treat you like dirt and turn you into collection agencies. Plus, modern medicine in the 1990s and early 2000s kept misdiagnosing me, giving me antibiotics for allergies and depression pills for ear infections and prescribed psychoanalysis for a vitamin D deficiency. It seemed clear, finally, based on the testimony of others, that the root of my decades and decades of struggle was gluten intolerance. (All those days of school missed in high school! The used-up sick leave! The inability to focus! The mood swings! The brain fog! The lifelong melancholy disguised by over-exuberance! The way I had to will myself to be productive, no matter how deeply I loved what I was doing.) Still it took another year—a year!—to completely phase gluten out of my diet. The delay was partly the result of my failure to believe that something so simple could be at the root of my troubles, and partly an unwillingness to give up certain foods.

During that year I did a considerable amount of research on gluten intolerance. It seemed the entire nation was focused on it. I hate fads and never take part in them, and I suspect my stubborn self was assuming its usual wait-and-see attitude. The problem was that I was spending every alone minute on the sofa, contracting every jagged virus that came along, and riding an energy roller coaster that escalated during my years of perimenopause, wreaking havoc on a number of relationships. Why? Because Phil and I had made a hobby of sampling microbrewed beer, and beer is nothing if not a vehicle for gluten.

The turning point came when I began looking at resources for folks who were gluten-intolerant and found that sometimes the only symptom, weird as it sounds, is left shoulder pain. Over the months I had developed left shoulder pain that was so bad, it kept me awake at night. And I couldn't predict it. No predicting the severity of it. I would have given up anything to be rid of that wicked pain.

A word of warning here: left arm, neck, and shoulder pain can be cardiac-related, so don't attempt to be your own diagnostician. But in my case, I knew that I had had a cardiac workup not too far back and that my ticker was pristine.

So, I finally, finally lived my first fully gluten-free week in June 2013. Funny thing: I worked circles around myself during those seven days. No fatigue. No naps. No disruption of night sleep. *No* shoulder pain. A year later—after a few trip-ups involving oats (see *The Grocery List* on page 29), tortilla chips (many are not gluten-free because the factories in which they are created also process wheat products), and French fries (fry grease used for anything but fresh-cut French fries can be contaminated with gluten)—I crossed the portal into gluten-free living and am experiencing a level of health unprecedented in my life. Now I am very careful. I am that little girl with the cupcake.

A NOTE ABOUT GLUTEN-FREE BAKING

By Jan Calvert, owner of Bridge Baking in Lewiston, Idaho

It was never my life's dream to open a bakery. In fact, I'm not sure it ever even crossed my mind until a couple of years ago. I was diagnosed as gluten-intolerant in 2007, ending two full years of increasingly debilitating "allergies," uncomfortable gastrointestinal issues, and fatigue. Extreme fatigue, as in, "How am I ever going to be able to support myself if I can't get off the sofa?" fatigue.

After several doctors prescribed every allergy tablet/pill/shot available at the time—and those didn't help in the slightest—a dear friend sent me to her naturopathic practitioner. I don't think I was in Dr. Pam's examination room more than ten minutes when she said, "You're horribly sensitive to wheat. Stop eating it. You'll feel better."

Three short days later, I absolutely couldn't believe it. I felt *good*. For the first time in more than two years, I felt great! I remember waking up one morning thinking, "Wow, I had completely forgotten what it feels like to have energy." And all because of one simple thing: avoiding wheat and gluten. It still amazes me that doing this one thing has made such a life-enhancing change for me.

Fast-forward to 2012. I moved from Portland, Oregon, to Lewiston, Idaho, to be closer to family. Portland had offered so many options for those seeking high-quality, gluten-free products, I never considered that these products might not be available everywhere. Turns out they're not—especially in areas such as northern Idaho and eastern Washington that produce a lot of wheat and other gluten-containing grain. There was nothing beyond the nationally-available commercial products found in many grocery stores (and a fairly limited supply of that). So, after a few weeks of settling in, I began noodling with the idea of starting a gluten-free baking service.

I've been a lifelong recreational baker—the person who's always asked to bring dessert to gatherings, never salad. And now it's come full circle: I'm doing the one thing I never considered but have always loved. There is nothing like the joy I feel when a customer walks in the door and says, "You mean I can eat anything in here? It's all safe?" Or when a young mom comes in, almost tearfully, asking if I can prepare a birthday cake for her child who has a long list of allergies/sensitivities, and she hears, "Of course it's possible." Having a gluten-free bakery is the most gratifying thing I've ever done.

WHAT IF YOU CAN TOLERATE GLUTEN?

Jan and I have talked at length about whether to include conversion information for readers who are *not* intolerant of gluten, but here is the thing: we both recommend using the recipes to explore both vegan and gluten-free options. Baking with gluten-free flours is so much more fun and interesting, and in many cases, you are supporting small growers and introducing into your diet an array of micronutrients not found in your basic five pound sack of regular flour. What I have found in my research—some of it dating back centuries—is that people have long noticed a relationship between wheat ingestion and an array of disorders. And most of the wheat grown today is not pure, but rather hybridized for high-yield and disease intolerance. Only a few heritage wheat strains remain.

I understand the nature of fads and that everyone these days seems to be on the gluten-free bandwagon, but that only tells me that these people suspect that it is possible to feel better than they do, and are willing to give everything a try. I have often wondered whether wheat is a good idea for any of us, and it concerns me that many environmental allergies may actually stem from undiagnosed sensitivity to or intolerance of the wheat plant itself—and not just gluten. Wheat is so ubiquitous, there is almost no way to know its effect on you unless you completely eliminate it and all processed foods from your diet for a period of time.

Both Jan and I have worked hard to get these recipes just right, but we have not proofed them with wheat flour. Plus, you can pick up any one of thousands of cookbooks off the shelf and find, say, a peanut butter cookie recipe that uses regular flour—although none will match Jan's for its flavor, texture, and nutritional value. If you still feel compelled to experiment with these recipes using wheat, however, the formula is this: take the total number of grams of grains and starches and divide by 140. This will give you the number of cups of unbleached wheat flour to use. Also eliminate the binders such as xanthan gum, guar gum, etc. Please understand that we absolutely have not tested these recipes for use with wheat flour, and we doubt the final outcome will compare.

ORGANIC FOODS AND THE DIRTY DOZEN

I find it sad and strange to live in a world in which unadulterated food is not the norm, rather it has to be labeled *organic*, has to be *certified*. I don't want to delve into it too much here, since the world is full of books and websites discussing the whys and wherefores of eating organic foods versus those treated with pesticides and fertilizers.

Instead, I'll just say that I have written this cookbook assuming that you are going to be purchasing organic foods or foods grown using organic processes (organic certification is too expensive for many small farmers) as much as possible. For the most part, all the recipes were created and tested using organic products. We keep a list on our refrigerator of the so-called "dirty dozen," as well as a list naming those fruits and vegetables with the least pesticide residue.

What we have found across the board, however, is that the flavor and texture is *always* superior in organically-grown produce because of the lack of chemical fertilizer, which makes fruits and vegetables grow too rapidly and too big. As much as possible, we buy from local farmers and growers in season and try very hard not to buy goods shipped from other countries, no matter the season. It makes no sense to me to pay for an apple to come half way around the world in the dark of winter. It does make sense to me to buy local and to either dry or preserve food so that we might enjoy it in the off-season.

I've labeled my list the "dirty baker's dozen" because I've included nuts, which are some of the worst repositories for pesticide residues.

The Dirty Baker's Dozen
- Apples
- Bell peppers
- Cherries
- Grapes
- Nectarines
- Nuts of all kinds
- Peaches
- Pears
- Potatoes
- Raspberries
- Soybeans (these are almost always genetically modified unless grown organically)
- Spinach
- Strawberries

Foods with the Lowest Pesticide Residues
- Asparagus
- Avocados
- Bananas
- Blueberries
- Broccoli
- Cauliflower
- Corn (most corn grown in this country is genetically-modified unless grown organically)
- Kiwi
- Mangoes
- Onions
- Papaya
- Pineapples
- Peas

INFLAMMATION AND DISEASE

Anyone who is alive and awake in the world today knows that the relationship between inflammation and disease process has been firmly established, and that we now understand that the source of inflammation is the food we eat. Low glycemic, processed food is the culprit, and our bodies wear themselves out trying to make use of what few nutrients this type of food contains.

Our natural ability to combat inflammation diminishes with age. Luckily for us, much evidence exists to indicate that disease process can be reversed by embracing a mostly raw, plant-based diet. For more information, see *Cool, Trustworthy Resources* at the back of the book. Also, if you research on your own, be careful of websites that are supported by meat and processed food industries, which take a decidedly biased stance.

Foods That Cause Inflammation

- Alcohol
- Dairy products
- Food additives
- Fried foods
- Gluten and wheat products
- Hydrogenated and trans-fats such as margarine, shortening, lard, and products made with them
- Iodized salt
- Meat and poultry (does not include wild-caught, high-fat fish such as salmon)
- Peanuts
- Processed, packaged, and prepared foods
- Synthetic sweeteners
- White sugar and sweets

Foods That Fight Inflammation

- Beets
- Berries
- Dark, leafy greens (such as kale and spinach)
- Fatty fish (such as salmon, mackerel, tuna, and sardines)
- Garlic and onions
- Ginger and turmeric
- Nuts (except peanuts)
- Olive oil
- Peppers
- Soy in the form of tofu and edamame (*not* soy-based processed foods)
- Tart cherries
- Tomatoes
- Whole grains (other than wheat, barley, and rye)

WHAT ABOUT GMO'S?

Hmmm. So certain entities don't want to be required to label the genetically modified foods they sell? And they spend millions of dollars on anti-labeling campaigns in states where it is put to the vote? And they are suing the state of Vermont where voters decided "no to GMOs; yes to GMO labeling"? Is that not suspicious? Consumer ignorance is a most frightening phenomenon in a capitalistic society.

Bottom line? Remember that most genetically-modified plants are designed to accommodate herbicides. If you eat that genetically modified food, you are eating weed-killer. Vote with your wallet: do not buy any food that is not specifically labeled non-GMO and, in the case of foods claiming to be organic, certified organic by Oregon Tilth. For more on this subject, see *Cool, Trustworthy Resources* on page 157.

IN THE PANTRY

You must be thinking—but isn't all this expensive? Well, it is and it isn't. It is true that organic fruits and vegetables can be more expensive than those that are "conventionally" grown, and retailers do take advantage of the fact that some of us are willing to pay an extra nickel if it means avoiding what we consider to be rather despicable growing practices. In our case, Phil and I began cooking more and more from scratch, eating raw, and buying most foods in bulk. We joined an organic food buying club which allows us to purchase directly from growers and wholesalers. We also preserve a small amount of our own food, and relish (pun intended) Phil's assortment of vegetable plots, which most summers keeps us supplied with tomatoes, peppers, and several herbs that we harvest and dry for use during the winter.

All in all, we now spend about fifty percent less on groceries than we did five years ago—even taking into account considerable inflation. All it took was changing our habits around food preparation and doing a little research and planning. In the end, we both also eat less because we are more satisfied, and that adds up, too.

If you're thinking you're too busy to be so focused on food and food preparation, give it a go for two weeks. Your increased energy levels more than make up for the time spent, and like everything else, once you've adapted, you won't be able to imagine life another way.

HONEY AND SWEETNESS

Some vegans don't eat honey because it is produced by a living, independently mobile being. I don't know how I feel about this other than to say, with concerns about bee colony collapse, it seems to me the more bee farmers the better, and if they keep bees to harvest honey, well, at least they are still keeping bees, and at least those bees are going about the business of pollinating the very plants we want to eat. Some recipes in this book do call for honey, but you can easily substitute agave syrup or rice syrup at your discretion.

Also, please keep in mind that much white sugar is made from genetically modified beets nowadays, so do be careful in your selection—go for organic cane sugar. It is more expensive, but we all need to limit the number of sweets we eat anyway, so make that your incentive and buy the good stuff.

Remember, too, that, as far as the body is concerned, sugar is sugar is sugar. Agave syrup is touted because it is primarily fructose and contains the fiber inulin, so it is more slowly digested, making it lower on the glycemic scale. However, even fructose eventually breaks down to glucose, so choose wisely and save the sweet treats for special occasions.

THAT PESKY EGG BUSINESS

Of course, going vegan means not using eggs in baking. Someday I hope to thank them in person, but it was Angela Liddon with her wonderful website *Oh She Glows*, Candace Walsh with *Great Gluten-Free Vegan Eats*, and Alexandra Jamieson with *Vegan Cooking for Dummies* who helped me over the hump.

Eggs serve three purposes in baking: leavening, binding, and providing moisture. Knowing the egg's role in the recipe is the secret to mastering substitutions. As with everything, I've studied and studied and come to my own conclusion and that is sometimes—*sometimes*—I am willing to sacrifice ethics for taste and texture. So despite the objections of other vegans and organic cooking websites, I regularly use xanthan gum in baked goods as a substitute for egg.

Here is the thing: xanthan gum comes from corn. No. It doesn't come from corn. It's created in a lab from the excrement of a bacterium that grows on corn. Corn grown in the U.S. is almost 100 percent genetically modified unless it's labeled organic. Bob's Red Mill does guarantee that the corn it uses is not genetically modified, but it is hard to find organic xanthan gum. Since it is a product of an organism—as with honey—and very highly processed, many vegans and those who stick to a raw foods diet won't use it. Also, some people are flat sensitive to it, suffering symptoms similar to those caused by gluten ingestion. Still others complain about after-taste and gumminess, which I've not experienced. Lastly, it's expensive, even if a little does go a long way.

Guar gum is similar, except that it comes from the guar bean, which grows in India. Once again, guar gum does not fall off the vine. It is a processed food that comes from a plant—a brick and mortar plant. It's in practically every processed food—if you've eaten store-bought ice cream, you've eaten guar gum. I haven't tried baking with it because most of what I've read says that it is a clumsy second to xanthan gum. Plus, guar gum has the effect of lowering blood sugar, so people—like my Phil—who are on a hypoglycemic for diabetes should avoid it. Besides, each of my recipes only uses a teaspoon or so of xanthan gum, and I've got an entire pound of the stuff in my fridge, and my down-home ethic requires me to use it until it's gone.

But here also is the thing for me: once in a blue moon I like to bake a batch of cookies, or a cake, or a loaf of bread. Not often—a few times a year. And when I do, I like those baked goods to be moist, highly textured, and substantial-bodied. I know I can accomplish that with other ingredients like agar agar (from seaweed) and chia seed, but I haven't gotten around to experimenting with those yet. When I do, I will let you know what I've decided.

Other ingredients substitute well for eggs; for example, applesauce or mashed banana in certain recipes—especially pancakes—works nicely. Ground flax seed (particularly golden flax) soaked in warm water is wonderful for binding muffins and cookies. I combine it with xanthan gum in my burger recipes, which are, as you might imagine, quite dense and really need that brute force combination to hold them together.

One note of caution—in gluten-free recipes you may run across the use of gelatin as a binder, but, as we all know, gelatin comes from horses and horses are not vegan, even if, as Phil says, the horses themselves are.

Here is a comprehensive breakdown of egg substitutes and what they do.

Agar Agar

Agar agar is a vegetarian gelatin is derived from algae or seaweed found in Southeast Asia, and it binds and thickens dough. It's used as an egg white substitute: dissolve one tablespoon plain agar powder in one tablespoon water for each egg. Whip, chill, and whip again before using.

Apple Cider Vinegar

Apple cider vinegar works as leavening only; it has no binding qualities. Mix one tablespoon apple cider vinegar with one teaspoon baking soda for each egg.

Applesauce, Avocado, Banana, or Pumpkin

These fruits are good as a binder. Substitute ¼ cup unsweetened applesauce (preferably homemade; see *Cherry Oat Sunday Cake* on page 45), banana, mashed avocado, or unsweetened pumpkin for each egg in quick breads, cornbread, cookies, muffins, and pancakes.

Cashews

Cashews can serve as an egg yolk substitute: Soak raw* cashews overnight in filtered water. Grind to a smooth cream using a high-powered blender. Replace each yolk with 1 ½ tablespoons cashew cream. *(*Technically speaking, cashews are not raw; see page 30).*

Chia Seeds

How many of us did not own a Chia Pet? Chia is part of the mint family, the seeds of which are a bounty of omega-3s and fiber. Ground seeds mixed with water become a gel that thickens, binds, and adds moisture in breads and pastries. One tablespoon ground seeds to three tablespoons of water substitutes for one egg; increase baking time by 15 minutes.

Chickpea Flour

High in protein, chickpea flour works both as a binder and as leavening. For each egg, mix three tablespoons chickpea flour with three tablespoons warm water, stirring until thick and creamy.

Coconut Milk

Full-fat canned coconut milk replaces egg yolks in custards for texture, body, and richness. Use one tablespoon plus one teaspoon coconut milk for each egg yolk.

Ener-G® Egg Replacer™

Ener-G® Egg Replacer™ is a commercial product and is just what it sounds like. Made from a combination of various starches and binders, it works especially well in baked goods. Its greatest advantage is ease of use. For each egg, use 1 ½ teaspoons in 2 tablespoons water.

Ground Flax Seed

Ground flax seed may be used for leavening and binding. The golden variety contains more oil and, to me, produces a tighter bind. It works well in baked goods of all kinds, pan breads, and pancakes. One tablespoon of ground seed to three tablespoons of warm water substitutes for one egg or one teaspoon xanthan gum; for an even stronger bind, boil the seed in water until a very thick gel forms.

Guar Gum

Guar gum functions as a binder and works well in creamy dishes and sauces. It also lowers bad cholesterol and blood sugar, but diabetics should use with caution. Please note that it can cause gas and constipation.

Psyllium Husk

You may recognize psyllium husk for its use as a digestive aid. It is very high in fiber (seven grams fiber in ten grams), and it is often prescribed for assistance with constipation and weight loss, so you may have to shop for it at a pharmacy. Many people who can't tolerate xanthan or guar gum find they do very well with psyllium. In baked goods, it holds and retains moisture and works nicely in recipes that rely on gluten, such as breads, pizza dough, rolls, and pasta. Mix 1 teaspoon psyllium husk to 3 tablespoons boiling water for each egg.

Silken Tofu

Silken tofu binds and adds moisture. One-quarter cup replaces one egg in cakes and quick breads; tofu must be well-blended and completely smooth before using.

Xanthan Gum

Use xanthan gum for binding and thickening, as it provides a somewhat elastic texture for breads and cakes. Replace each egg with one teaspoon xanthan gum.

No matter which substitute you decide to try, start by using the same amount as you would egg or xanthan gum. For example, if you have a recipe that calls for two eggs or two teaspoons of xanthan gum, substitute two teaspoons of your preferred replacement (except for flax and chia seed; see instructions above). Finding your own path will take patience and practice, but, as with all things of an experimental nature, the outcome will be worth the journey.

COCONUT OIL NATION

I am in love with coconut oil. With each dietary transition Phil and I have made, we have seen noticeable changes in our bodies, but not since we discovered hemp seed have we been as affected as we have by coconut oil. Our skin, hair, gums, and nails have taken on a healthy glow, and I'm convinced that coconut oil is the cause of it, even if the scientific jury is still out on the subject.

We use pure, extra virgin, organic coconut oil and purchase in bulk. Extra-virgin coconut oil is not hydrogenated, but it is a saturated fat—ninety-two percent. Despite what media hype and 1990s-style fad diets might lead you to believe, the truth is that our bodies do need small amounts of saturated fat every day for hormone production, cellular membrane function, and other cell duties. In fact, it turns out that about ten percent of fat calories every day should come from saturated fat. For most of us that's about 11–14 grams a day, or about one tablespoon.

The wondrous thing about coconut oil is that, unlike animal fat, it contains no cholesterol, but it does feature an unusual composition of short and medium chain fatty acids—lauric (forty-four percent) and myristic (16.8 percent). These fatty acids not only appear to positively affect the balance of good (HDL) and bad (LDL) cholesterols in the body, but are also metabolized relatively quickly in much the same way as complex carbohydrates, so they are less likely to be stored as adipose tissue—a fancy medical term for body fat.

What I love about cooking with coconut oil is that it handles very high temperatures; it hardens at room temperature, so it adds texture to baked goods; it makes the lightest, fluffiest popcorn I have ever tasted; and it makes fried foods—tofu and tempeh at our house—come out wonderfully crispy and with the faintest of coconut flavor. We don't use much fat in cooking, but if we do, it's likely coconut oil.

A NOTE ABOUT GLUTEN-FREE FLOURS AND FLOUR BLENDS

By Jan Calvert, owner of Bridge Baking in Lewiston, Idaho

As you have probably discovered, many gluten-free flour blends are available commercially, each of which claim to be the only flour mix you'll need. Many of them are very good, but I've discovered two things about commercially-prepared flour blends: in gluten-free baking, there is no such thing as one-size-fits-all; and when compared to making it yourself, store-bought blends are expensive. Also, commercial products often contain a lot of rice flour, which translates to dry, gritty baked goods.

It's taken a couple of years of trial and error—with *lots* of errors along the way—but I've come to truly enjoy how gluten-free baking involves so many choices. "Regular" bakers use few flours, primarily all-purpose white flour. But we have so many options. Want it moister? Substitute in some millet or sorghum flour. A little sturdier? Use oat flour. An earthy, "whole grain" flavor? Use buckwheat or teff. More tender? Add almond meal.

Unfortunately, as you also likely know, gluten-free baking is expensive. No on-sale-$3.99-for-ten-pound sacks of flour for us. And xanthan and guar gum? Yikes. It is my desire to give you recipes that work every time, and to eliminate "mistakes" that are too crumbly to eat but too expensive to toss out.

One method to increase your chances for success is to *weigh everything*—especially the gluten-free flours. Don't spoon and scoop into a measuring cup, but rather *weigh* every particle in grams. Why? Because the per-cup weight of gluten-free flours varies widely, and being off by a tablespoon or so can make the difference between success and another doorstop brick.

For example, a tablespoon of white rice flour weighs a little over nine grams. So if you measure a cup of white rice flour but pack it a bit more tightly than I do, an extra tablespoon increases the amount by six percent—which may not be enough to change the outcome of the baked product significantly. But that same extra tablespoon of almond meal increases the amount by over fifteen percent. Gluten-free vegan baking already involves a lot of variables, so it's much more cost-effective to reduce the guesswork whenever possible. And then there's my favorite advantage of weighing over measuring—no more trying to scrape the last bit of peanut butter out of a measuring cup!

So go out and buy yourself a digital scale. Things to look for: is the display positioned so you can see the read-out even if there is a large bowl on the scale? Will it convert from grams to ounces? Is there a "tare" function (very important), so you can zero out the weight without starting over each time you add another ingredient? Is the weight capacity of the scale at least ten pounds, enough to accommodate your largest mixing bowl full of ingredients? You should be able to find one that will work for you for no more than thirty-five dollars. That's not inexpensive—but you'll save the cost in fewer baking flops.

If you plan to make bread, consider one more investment that will ensure consistent results: a digital probe thermometer. Breads that lack gluten don't "thump" well when they're done—the traditional test for normal breads. So it's more reliable to go by temperature. A digital probe thermometer has a read-out that sits on the counter and is connected via a long cable to a temperature probe that you push into the bread. The thermometer can be set to sound a buzzer when the probe reaches the correct temperature. You should be able to find one for about twenty dollars.

Back to "no such thing as one size fits all": a large part of successful gluten-free baking is finding the correct ratio of grains to starches in the flour mix. Baked goods that are denser, such as muffins, have more grain than starch in the flour blend. But to create a light, crunchy cracker, the flour blend needs to have more starch than grain.

All gluten-free flours are either a grain or a starch, and the challenge is to create the right proportion of each to mimic the strength and structure found in gluten. I've found that having three different blends on hand does the trick nearly every time: one that is seventy percent grain and thirty percent starch, another that is fifty percent of each, and the last that is thirty-five percent grain and sixty-five percent starch. All of these blends are by weight, not volume.

If you bake frequently, it's easiest to throw a batch of each blend together and keep them on hand in air-tight containers. Or you can create a blend for each recipe as you make it. For the math-challenged among you, just consider this your chance to finally conquer the calculator!

There are no rules in creating your blends, just a couple of guidelines. One is to keep the total weight of rice flours, either brown or white, to no more than sixty-five percent of the total weight of the grains, to reduce the grittiness that is common in commercially prepared gluten-free baked goods. For example, if you need 150 grams of a 70/30 blend, the weight of the grains portion of the blend will be 105 grams, or seventy percent of 150. Of that, keep the total of white and brown rice flours to no more than sixty-eight grams out of the 105 grams.

The other guideline is to use at least two starches. Continuing with the example above, you'll need a total of forty-five grams of starch, which is thirty percent of the 150 grams. Divide those forty-five grams between two or three starches: fifteen grams each of potato starch, tapioca starch, and cornstarch. Sensitive to corn? Replace the cornstarch with arrowroot, or use twenty grams of potato starch and twenty-five grams of tapioca starch.

To create your own blends, simply keep these guidelines in mind and make your selections from the lists below. Weigh out each type of flour into a large bowl and whisk them together. Whisk again. Better yet, toss it all into a food-grade two-gallon bucket, put on the lid, and shake like crazy—whatever it takes to make sure the mixture is thoroughly blended. I usually make a total of 1000 grams of each blend at a time, which is roughly seven cups.

Grains

- Almond meal/flour
- Amaranth
- Brown rice
- Buckwheat
- Coconut (use sparingly in a blend: no more than fifteen percent of the total grains, as it soaks up moisture like crazy)
- Corn flour or masa harina
- Millet
- Oat flour (be sure it's certified gluten-free)
- Potato flour (not to be confused with potato starch)
- Quinoa flour
- Sorghum (also called sweet white sorghum)
- Teff

Starches

- Arrowroot
- Cornstarch
- Potato starch (not to be confused with potato flour)
- Tapioca starch (sometimes called tapioca flour)
- Sweet white rice (also called glutinous rice, which is not to be confused with gluten or mochiko)

Below, you'll find the flour blends that are used at Bridge Baking and in the *From the Bakery* recipe section of this book (see page 129).

70/30

Grains

100 grams white rice flour
100 grams oat flour
150 grams millet
175 grams brown rice flour
175 grams sorghum
700 grams total

Starches

150 grams potato starch
75 grams tapioca starch
75 grams cornstarch
300 grams total

50/50

Grains

150 grams sorghum
100 grams almond meal
200 grams brown rice flour
50 grams oat flour
500 grams total

Starches

200 grams sweet rice flour
100 grams potato starch
100 grams tapioca starch
100 grams cornstarch
500 grams total

35/65

Grains

200 grams brown rice flour
100 grams sorghum
50 grams potato flour
350 grams total

Starches

250 grams sweet rice flour
150 grams potato starch
150 grams tapioca starch
100 grams cornstarch
650 grams total

AN ADDENDUM FROM PAULA: *While I've converted my measurements for baked goods recipes to weight in grams, I have not done so for cooked foods. The reasons are simple: either the weight difference in small amounts (in a tablespoon, say) is negligible, or the weight variations do not impact outcomes the way they do in baked goods. When I found out all bakers normally weigh their flour instead of measuring, it was as though a great puzzle piece fell into place for me. One of my life's mysteries was why bread never came out the same way twice—if it came out at all. With the money I've spent on botched baking experiments over the years, I could retire. Discovering this trick is like being reborn.*

THE GROCERY LIST

In addition to the flours and starches on Jan's list and the aforementioned egg substitutes, I keep the following items in my pantry. Remember, as much as possible, buy organic. I'm convinced that, in the long run, it will save money on doctor bills, and, as noted earlier, because food tastes better and is more satisfying, you may be inclined to eat less. The latter is not a promise, though!

Oils

Buy only expeller-pressed oils which are not chemically or heat-derived, as other oils are. When you are out buying your scale and temperature probe, buy yourself a Misto® sprayer or nonstick spray with a pump applicator. Never use nonstick spray containing propellants.

- Coconut oil
- Extra-virgin olive oil

- Peanut oil
- Sesame oil
- Sunflower oil
- Toasted sesame oil

Nuts and Seeds

- Almonds

    Tannins in raw almonds can cause gastrointestinal distress. To get rid of these, soak almonds overnight and dry them in a dehydrator or oven at 150 degrees for twelve hours or so. Soaking in this fashion results in a sweeter nut and releases beneficial enzymes.

- Cashews

    Cashews are not raw, nor are they a nut. Rather, they are a seed protruding from the cashew fruit, in a pod filled with a caustic substance which must be burned off before it is edible.

- Flax seed

    As mentioned previously, I find golden flax seed creates a more gelatinous "egg."

- Hazelnuts
- Hemp seed

    We could improve world health if each person ate two tablespoons of hemp seed daily. See my inclusion of hemp protein powder in the In the Fridge *section on page 32 and read more about the unparalleled nutritional power of hemp seed and hemp protein in* Blue Moon Vegetarian.

- Pecans
- Quinoa

    Even though we use it like a grain, quinoa is actually a seed from a plant that is a relative of spinach and beets. I especially like the texture and flavor of quinoa pasta.

- Sunflower Seeds
- Walnuts

Dried Beans

- Black beans
- Black-eyed peas
- Chickpeas (also called garbanzo beans)
- Kidney beans
- Lentils (French green, brown, yellow, and/or baby brown)
- Mung beans
- Pinto beans
- Navy beans
- White beans

Grains

- Brown basmati rice

    I love the texture and flavor of basmati over other rice varieties; I also keep a supply of several types of store-bought brown rice pasta.

- Oats

    These should be gluten-free, of course; the issue is not so much that oats contain a great amount of gluten, but that they are frequently processed alongside wheat.

- Millet
- White basmati rice

Other

- Arrowroot powder
- Baking powder

    Buy only aluminum-free, as ingestion of aluminum has been associated with Alzheimer's disease.

- Baking soda
- Chickpea flour (also called garbanzo flour)
- Coconut milk (canned and full-fat)
- Coconut sugar

    This is also sometimes called palm sugar and is a fine substitute for brown sugar.

- Dried fruits
- Herbs

    These are best when you grow them yourself and use them fresh; second best is to grow your own and dry them; third is to buy fresh from the supermarket and use right away, and then dry the rest; last place should be buying organic dried herbs in bulk from a food co-op or online from folks who grow, process, and package the herbs themselves. Fresh herbs have medicinal properties. By the time they get to you in those little brand-name jars, they don't pack much wallop, even as flavoring.

- Organic cane sugar

    In winter, which is when I tend to bake, I also buy organic brown sugar and organic powdered sugar. I don't bake with beet sugar because of the heavy concentration of pesticides in root crops and because of the high incidence of genetically-modified beets grown in this country. I want cane sugar, and I want to know it has been nurtured by small-scale growers.

- Sea salt

    Try sea salt from different sources until you find one you like the best. I keep both plain and alder smoked sea salt, since I like the deep notes that the smoked variety lends to certain dishes.

- Spices

    Like herbs, these are better fresh, but not many of us are going to grow a nutmeg tree. Try to find a good source, such as your food co-op, where you can trust the freshness and the quality.

- Tony Chachere's® Original Creole Seasoning

    We love this stuff and use it on everything, and you will, too.

- Vegetable bouillon
- Yellow split pea flour

In the Fridge

- Coconut aminos

    This is a great gluten-free substitute for Worcestershire sauce.

- Coconut milk beverage

    I prefer the unsweetened version by the brand So Delicious®, and they also make delectable coconut milk ice cream and yogurt.

- Extra-firm tofu

    Freeze first, and then thaw before using for a more meaty texture. Tofu contains a lot of water, so be sure to press out as much as you can before using. Also, there is some discussion about whether too much tofu is good for a person: some components are thought to be hard on the thyroid, and it does contain certain estrogens that are biologically identical to those our bodies produce. Because of this, you may notice that most of the recipes in this book that feature tofu use a very small amount. We limit ourselves to about twelve ounces of tofu each per month. And about once a month we may share an order of steamed edamame (soybeans in the pod) at one of our local restaurants. As with everything, do your homework and do what works best for you. Also, don't forget that most soybeans grown in our country are genetically modified. Be certain you buy only tofu or soybeans that are certified organic by Oregon Tilth (Oregon Tilth certification verifies that the strictest level of organic farming practices have been maintained—see "Cool, Trustworthy Resources" on page 157).

- Firm tofu

    Use this tofu in recipes as is; do not freeze.

- Hemp protein

    As mentioned earlier, I feature a discussion on hemp protein in Blue Moon Vegetarian *and don't want to duplicate it here. But the upshot is that hemp seed features the highest-quality plant protein and is a complete protein—meaning it includes all nine essential amino acids. Also high in fiber, it contains perfectly balanced ratios of omega-3 and -6 and has been shown to reduce inflammation.*

- Jams and preserves

- Hot pepper sauce

    We keep several kinds: cayenne (also known as Louisiana Red), habanero, and jalapeño.

- Ketchup

    We like small-batch brands such as Portland Ketchup.

- Miso
- Nut butters
- Nutritional yeast

    This is not actual yeast that you would use in baking, but rather a by-product; even with a yeast allergy, I tolerate it just fine. Use this whenever you want to add cheese flavor to a recipe, or blend it into tofu with a little sea salt to create a cheese replacement.

- Pepper sauce
- Prepared mustard
- Silken tofu

    See Extra-firm tofu above.

- Sparkling mineral water
- Tahini

    The moment I don't have tahini (sesame seed butter) on hand is the moment I will have a painful and unrelenting craving for hummus.

- Tamari sauce

    Tamari is gluten-free soy sauce. We only use the low-sodium variety these days.

- Tamarind paste

    This brings a tangy undertone to south-of-the-border dishes.

- Tempeh

    We eat a lot of tempeh and prefer Tofurky® brand (Turtle Island Foods) because of its mixture of sprouted seeds. It's great to bake, fry, or grill for a main course, or to use as the focus of a sandwich. You can also crumble and use it in recipes that call for a meaty texture.

- Vegenaise®

    We know even omnivores who love Vegenaise®. I could never go back to those national mayonnaise brands, and I hope the Follow Your Heart® company never sells out.

When I was younger, every time I bought a new cookbook I immediately ran out and bought a bunch of items on the "what to stock in your pantry" list and then ended up never using them. Now I browse through the entire cookbook armed with sticky tabs or paper clips, choose a handful of the most intriguing recipes, mark them for safekeeping, and shop for ingredients just for those recipes. It takes the pressure off: I don't have to change my life completely; I just want to try a new recipe or two.

I also recommend looking up books and websites from the resource section at the end of this book (see page 157). Nothing serves you better than a bit of education, and we live in an age when we are able to easily find every manner of information about every subject. Read about hemp protein. Read about gluten intolerance. Read about the vegan life. Read about how to generate less waste. Read about how to grow your own tomatoes on your apartment balcony.

SIPS AND SMOOTHIES

Giving up commercially-prepared soda pop is a good first step toward improved health. But that doesn't mean we have to limit ourselves to water, although getting enough of that is equally important. I believe liquid refreshment can be just as restorative as good food and I've provided a few examples here to prove it.

PHIL'S DAILY HEMP SHAKE

2 medium-sized bananas

2 cups berries, mango, or other fresh fruit

1 cup washed and torn kale or spinach, loosely packed

4 tablespoons hemp powder

½ cup plain coconut milk yogurt

1 cup unsweetened coconut milk beverage

2 cups sparkling mineral water (I like San Pellegrino®)

This is what we take to work every day—and nothing else. A quart-sized glass jar of it is just enough for lunch and snacks. Phil lost about twenty-five pounds the first year he did this, which was the year before we switched to vegetarianism. I haven't been so lucky, but we both agree that this is the change that made us recognize the relationship between food and health and taught us that hemp protein is one of our most potent nutritional sources.

Chop bananas and/or other fruit and add to blender with yogurt and coconut milk. Add hemp powder and blend for at least 2 minutes. Add sparkling water and blend for 1 minute. Adjust the ingredients to suit individual taste. Makes approximately two quarts.

CHOCOLATE CHAI SMOOTHIE

4 tea bags Organic India® Tulsi Masala Chai

2 cups fresh coconut milk or refrigerated coconut milk beverage (not canned)

¼ cup canned coconut milk

2 bananas

3 tablespoons grated dark chocolate (I like Green & Black's® Organic)

2 tablespoons coconut sugar

1 teaspoon vanilla extract

4 cups ice

Pinch sea salt

Vegan chocolate syrup (I like Santa Cruz)

I created this one day when I craved *something* but didn't know what. Homemade chai is wonderful, but I'm still perfecting mine, and for this recipe I prefer Organic India's®' version.

Place glasses in freezer. Heat coconut milk beverage to boiling over medium heat. Add teabags. Remove from heat and steep 15 minutes. Add chocolate and stir to melt. Remove teabags and allow mixture to cool. Add mixture to blender with chopped banana, vanilla, coconut sugar, and ice. Blend until smooth. Drizzle the inside of prepared glasses with chocolate syrup. Serve immediately. Makes 3 16-ounce servings.

TOASTED COCONUT MOCHA FRAPPUCINO

12 ounces strong coffee, slightly warm

3 tablespoons grated chocolate (I like Green & Black's® Organic)

3 tablespoons coconut sugar

1 teaspoon coconut extract

1 teaspoon high-quality vanilla extract

1 cup canned coconut milk

Pinch alder smoked sea salt

4 cups ice

Toasted coconut

Chocolate shavings

We were shooting photographs for this book when I told the photographer that I had never tried a mocha or a Frappuccino®, so I decided to see what I could come up with. The original recipe included pulverized toasted coconut, but that made the concoction just a little too grainy. This one is rich and exotic.

To toast coconut, grate fresh coconut and dry in the oven at 200 degrees. Once dry, toast in the oven at 275 degrees until light brown.

Combine warm coffee, coconut sugar, and chocolate in blender and process on high for several minutes. Add both extracts, coconut milk, and sea salt and blend for several more minutes. Crush ice and add to blender, and then use the whip feature to process for 3–5 minutes. Garnish with toasted coconut and grated chocolate. Serve immediately. Makes 2 servings.

FUZZY TEA

1 quart filtered water

6 bags Organic India® Tulsi

1 quart sparkling mineral water

Phil is the master of recipe names, and as you will notice, some of them are a bit silly—those are where my poetry and his sense of humor merge. The name for Fuzzy Tea came about one Saturday morning when I said, "I have to remember to include Fizzy Tea in the cookbook." He said, making a joke, "Don't you mean Fuzzy Tea?" Not to be outdone, I said, "Why yes. Fuzzy Tea is exactly what I mean." And the name stuck. Tulsi is another word for holy basil, which is a medicinal herb known to be beneficial for an array of conditions, and when it's conjoined with green tea, as it is in the Organic India brand, it also is a stress-reliever. It's my favorite, favorite thing for getting through the 100-degree days we are prone to here at the mouth of Hell's Canyon.

Place tea bags and filtered water in a ½-gallon glass jar with the lid screwed on, and then place the jar in the sun for several hours. Remove tea bags, squeezing as much liquid out of them as possible. Add sparkling mineral water to tea and stir briefly, pouring over ice. Store in refrigerator with lid sealed tightly. Keeps for up to a week when refrigerated. Makes 4 servings.

DAY AT THE BEACH

2 cups unsweetened organic cranberry juice

Juice from 1 grapefruit

Agave syrup to taste

Juice from ½ lime

4 cups crushed ice

1 cup sparkling mineral water

1 lime, sliced

This recipe was inspired by a drink made at Pelicano, a wharfside fine dining establishment in Ilwaco, Washington, on the Long Beach Peninsula, which also is home to a number of cranberry bogs. While touring the area, we learned that commercial bogs are treated with pesticides and most bottled cranberry juice is made from concentrate—a puny replica of the real deal. Organic, small-batch, unsweetened, unfiltered cranberry juice is where all the love is, and let me tell you, it will rock your world. Please don't tell my mother, but the drink at Pelicano included a dose of 100 percent agave tequila blanco, which goes equally well with the recipe below.

Combine first four ingredients in blender and process briefly to blend. Add ice and combine using ice crush feature. Add sparkling mineral water and blend briefly. Pour into 10-ounce glasses and, if desired, add 1 ounce tequila blanco and stir. Garnish with sliced lime. Makes 4–6 servings.

BLUEBERRY-GINGER FIZZ

3 – 4 cups fresh blueberries, well mashed

2 tablespoons organic cane sugar

Juice from ½ small lemon

2 tablespoons fresh ginger, grated

Ice

Sparkling mineral water

Extra whole fresh blueberries

Additional lemon wedges

Agave syrup

Hendricks® gin*

Candied ginger

We have a hangout in downtown Clarkston known as Hogan's. It's a fixture that's been in the same place for decades, and when you step inside, you'd swear you were in downtown Chicago rather than the American outback. No TV. Lots of interesting photos and bawdy memorabilia. It's a spot where artists, musicians, poets, writers, academics, and other professionals and locals gather for dinner, libations, and great regional music. Kaitlyn Bergman, who we have known for years, has a gift for crafting drinks, and she graciously shared several of her "secret" recipes with me, starting with this one.

Bring berries, sugar, and lemon juice to a boil. Add ginger. Remove from heat, cover, and steep for 1 hour. Strain through a fine mesh strainer, discarding or composting pulp.

For each drink, place 5–6 blueberries in the bottom of a 10-ounce glass and fill with ice. Shake together 1 ounce Hendricks® gin, 1 lemon wedge, squeezed, 1 tablespoon agave syrup, and 2 ounces of blueberry mixture. Pour over ice, and top with sparkling water. Garnish with candied ginger. Makes enough blueberry mixture for 10–12 cocktails.

*Other gins are too piney.

VIOLET-PEACH PERSUASION

¼ cup filtered water

¼ cup organic cane sugar

2 pounds peaches

Hendricks®* gin or favorite vodka

Lemon wedges

Simple syrup

Violet syrup

Candied violets**

Another one of Kaitlyn's recipes, but Phil gets credit for naming it. The violet syrup is made by Monin, the Italian soda folks.

Make simple syrup by bringing equal parts water and sugar to a boil in a small saucepan. Remove from heat and allow to cool before using. Blanch peaches by placing in a metal strainer and briefly submerging in boiling water. Transfer immediately to a bowl or kettle filled with ice water. Remove skins and seeds, placing fruit in blender. Puree until smooth.

For each drink, fill a 10-ounce glass with ice. Add 1 ounce gin or vodka and the juice from 2–3 lemon wedges, or to taste. Add ½ ounce simple syrup and ½ cap violet syrup. Top with about ¼ cup peach puree. Garnish with several pieces of candied violet. Serve immediately. Makes enough peach puree and simple syrup for 6–8 drinks.

*Other gins are too piney.
**Can be ordered from www.Monin.com/en-gb/products/premium-syrups/monin-violet-syrup

MALLORY'S LAVENDER DREAM

1 cup filtered water

1 cup organic cane sugar

1 cup lavender buds

Cazadores® Reposado*

Sparkling mineral water

Lavender stalks

Mallory Fry earned her chops tending bar in New Orleans and also works at Hogan's. I'd love to include several of her drinks here, but I fear my mother can only take so much. This is one of my favorites: an amazing intersection of lavender and reposado tequila that is such a surprise.

Make lavender simple syrup by bringing equal parts water and sugar to a boil in a small saucepan. Remove from heat and add lavender buds. Cover and steep for 1 hour. Strain.

For each drink, fill a 10-ounce glass with ice. Add 2 ounces lavender simple syrup and 1 ounce reposado. Top with sparkling water. Garnish with lavender stalk. Makes enough simple syrup for 6–8 servings.

This particular reposado has just the right flavor to highlight the lavender.

GOOD MORNING

I doubt many of us jump up in the a.m. and start cooking breakfast, but at my house on weekends we do, and pretty much all of these recipes came from that inclination. I remember my mother and grandmothers getting up early every morning to create huge breakfasts. Now I'm lucky during the work week if I even grab a bowl of oatmeal. I'm pretty sure we are all the worse for this change in culture, and I for one wish we would restore the morning mealtime to our habits. There is a reason the word evolved: our bodies benefit all day long from "breaking the fast."

BLUE MOON BISCUITS AND GRAVY

BISCUITS

95 grams almond flour

46 grams chickpea flour

74 grams white rice flour

1 teaspoon baking powder

1 teaspoon baking soda

1 teaspoon organic cane sugar

½ teaspoon sea salt

½ teaspoon xanthan gum

⅓ cup coconut oil

½ teaspoon apple cider vinegar

Unsweetened coconut milk beverage or almond milk

Anyone who hails from Kentucky and southern Indiana has soda biscuits and milk gravy in her veins. I thought I'd have to give it up until I discovered the thickening properties of white rice flour and the way coconut oil mimics lard. Still, you can't deny that gravy is full of fat, so I do save this recipe for special occasions, mainly Sunday mornings in the heart of winter. I've also included a variation called Red-Eye Gravy, a phenomenon of the old West born of hard times and short rations, I'm guessing. I really love its deep, rich flavor and the lift from that jolt of coffee.

TO MAKE THE BISCUITS: Preheat oven to 375 degrees. Sift together all dry ingredients in a large bowl. Cut in coconut oil using pastry cutter, knives, or crumble by hand until mixture is coarse but evenly textured. Mix cider vinegar in ¼ cup of the milk. Add to flour mixture and mix by hand. Continue mixing in small amounts of the milk until a soft dough forms. Avoid kneading or overworking the dough. Allow dough to rest in bowl for 5 minutes. Roll out to ¾" thickness on floured board. Cut with biscuit cutter, re-rolling dough scraps until all is used up. Bake on ungreased cookie sheet for 15 minutes or until biscuits are golden brown. Makes 1 dozen biscuits.

GRAVY

2 tablespoons coconut oil

2 tablespoons white rice flour

1 ½ – 2 cups unsweetened coconut milk beverage

1 teaspoon garlic granules

2 tablespoons nutritional yeast

2 teaspoons vegan butter

⅛ teaspoon coconut aminos

Sea salt to taste

Fresh cracked black pepper to taste

TO MAKE THE GRAVY: Heat oil in a small skillet or saucepan over low heat. Add flour ½ tablespoon at a time, whisking as you go to make a paste of the oil. Add coconut milk a few tablespoons at a time, whisking to keep from lumping, until a gravy thickness is achieved. Stir in remaining ingredients and season to taste. Makes approximately 2 cups of gravy.

Variation: Red-Eye Gravy

Toast flour to a medium brown by stirring over low heat in a dry skillet before using. Substitute 1 cup of coffee for 1 cup of coconut milk. Add Louisiana Red Hot Sauce to taste.

CHERRY OAT SUNDAY CAKE

APPLESAUCE

3 medium-sized honeycrisp apples (I've tried other types of apples, but none compare)

2 cups filtered spring water

1 ½ cups coconut sugar

CAKE

2 flax eggs (see page 24)

3 cups whole gluten-free oats

124 grams sorghum flour

74 grams potato flour

28 grams tapioca flour

1 teaspoon xanthan gum

1 teaspoon ground cinnamon

1 teaspoon baking powder

1 teaspoon baking soda

1 teaspoon sea salt

1 cup unsweetened coconut milk beverage

½ cup agave syrup

½ cup sunflower oil

1 banana, pureed

2 cup frozen organic dark cherries

My mother sometimes made coffee cake, which was basically a many-egged yellow cake with a brown-sugar-and-butter-and-cinnamon crust on top. This is really more of a quick bread, and much more nutritious, but for me, there is no getting around the fact that Sunday mornings do occasionally call for cake. The texture and moisture of this one improves greatly after being refrigerated overnight, so do yourself a real favor and make it before going to bed.

TO MAKE THE APPLESAUCE: Peel, core, and coarsely chop apples. Place apples, water, and ½ cup coconut sugar in medium-sized slow cooker on low and cook 8–10 hours, stirring occasionally. The thickness of the applesauce at this point depends on the juiciness of the apples. If it needs to further thicken, remove lid and continue to cook on low until desired consistency is reached. Let cool and then spoon into canning jars, about ⅔ full. Makes about 3 cups. Set aside 1 cup applesauce. Store remaining applesauce in refrigerator for up to 1 month. It freezes beautifully for up to a year.

TO MAKE THE CAKE: Prepare flax eggs and set aside. Preheat oven to 350 degrees. Spray a 9" x 12" pan with sunflower oil and set aside. Blend remaining dry ingredients in a large mixing bowl. In a separate bowl, blend wet ingredients with 1 cup applesauce. Then stir into dry mixture. Continue stirring for 5 minutes. Mixture should be somewhat foamy. Add frozen cherries. Fold into batter until cherries are well distributed. Cover bowl with a slightly dampened towel and let batter sit for 15 minutes. Pour into prepared pan. Cover again and let sit another 15 minutes. Bake at 350 degrees for 1 hour or until inserted toothpick comes out clean. Allow to cool before serving. Makes 8–12 servings.

PHIL'S MELLOW YELLOW SCRAMBLE

1 tablespoon vegan butter

1 tablespoon toasted sesame oil

8 ounces silken tofu

2 tablespoons canned coconut milk

¼ cup plain coconut milk yogurt

½ yellow bell pepper, chopped

1 small yellow winter squash, chopped

2 cloves garlic, minced

3 tablespoons nutritional yeast

¼ teaspoon prepared mustard

1 teaspoon xanthan gum

2 flax eggs (see page 24)

½ teaspoon alder smoked sea salt

Fresh ground black pepper to taste

Tony Chachere's® Original Creole Seasoning to taste

A favorite from *Blue Moon Vegetarian*, this recipe originally featured a number of eggs, but you won't miss them at all.

Prepare flax eggs and set aside. Melt butter with oil in a skillet. Beat tofu with milk and yogurt and pour into skillet. Add vegetables and garlic and cook until vegetables are just starting to soften. Stir in yeast, mustard, xanthan gum, and flax eggs. Sprinkle with seasonings and continue tossing and stirring until cooked through and brown at the edges. Vegetables will be slightly firm. Add more seasoning to taste. Makes 6 servings.

SKILLET CAKES

2 flax eggs (see page 24)

92 grams chickpea flour

111 grams oat flour

95 grams almond meal

74 grams white rice flour

1 teaspoon baking soda

2 heaping tablespoons hemp powder

1 teaspoon cardamom

½ cup sunflower oil

½ cup unsweetened coconut milk beverage

½ cup plain yogurt

1 cup sparkling mineral water

This is a hearty, tender pancake that even pleased my grandchildren. You can make the dry mix in batches, but because of the hemp powder, be sure to store it in the fridge.

Prepare flax egg and set aside. In a large bowl, mix together all three flours and almond meal. Stir in the baking soda, hemp powder, and cardamom. In a separate small bowl, combine the sunflower oil, milk, yogurt, and eggs. Pour the liquid mixture into the dry mixture. Add enough sparkling water to make a thick batter. Cook on an oiled griddle over low heat until browned on both sides and cooked through. Makes 8–10 6-inch pancakes.

FRAGRANT PANCAKES

2 flax eggs (see page 24)

½ cup coconut oil

92 grams chickpea flour

65 grams brown rice flour

74 grams white rice flour

65 grams millet flour

¼ teaspoon ground lavender

¼ teaspoon ground cardamom

½ teaspoon baking soda

½ teaspoon xanthan gum

½ teaspoon sea salt

1 tablespoon coconut sugar

1 large banana, pureed

1 tablespoon high-quality vanilla extract

1 cup canned coconut milk

Sparkling mineral water

You can tell we have a thing for lavender. It grows like crazy in our arid region, and we have plenty of it in our garden. The lavender, cardamom, and vanilla calm and restore energy.

Prepare flax eggs and set aside. Melt coconut oil over low heat. Combine all dry ingredients in a bowl. Stir in banana, oil, and vanilla. Add coconut milk and enough sparkling water to create a somewhat thin- to medium-bodied batter, or as preferred. Batter may thicken as it sits. Continue adding sparkling water as necessary.

Brush griddle with oil prior to each batch. Preheat griddle over medium heat. Pour ¼–⅓ cup of batter for each pancake. Cook over medium heat until toasty brown and visibly cooked through. Flip and continue cooking until toasty brown. Serve with nut or seed butters and jam, warm agave syrup, or maple syrup. Makes 12 6" pancakes.

BRUNCH FLORENTINE

2 flax eggs (see page 24)

3 – 4 slices ½" thick sourdough bread*

8 ounces silken tofu

3 cloves garlic, minced

½ teaspoon Tony Chachere's® Original Creole Seasoning

2 cups baby spinach, washed and chopped

¼ cup green chili sauce

¼ cup canned coconut milk

¼ cup cashew milk

1 cup Can't Be Cheese (see page 95) or grated vegan cheddar cheese

2 teaspoons xanthan gum

This is another favorite recipe from *Blue Moon Vegetarian*. Once again, we omitted the eggs—6 of them!—in favor of a small amount of tofu.

Prepare flax eggs and set aside. Arrange bread in a buttered 9" x 13" baking dish. Mix all other ingredients except cheese in a medium-sized bowl and pour over bread. Top with crumbled cheese. Cover and let sit in refrigerator overnight. Bake the next morning at 350 degrees for 45 minutes. Allow to cool for 15 minutes after removing from oven. Makes 8 servings.

Bread should be homemade or artisan bread, gluten-free, of course, and several days old, not fresh. Bagged bread from a grocery store will simply dissolve.

PUMPKIN PUDDING

3 flax eggs (see page 24)

1 15-ounce can of pumpkin

3 ounces silken tofu

½ cup organic cane sugar

1 teaspoon xanthan gum

⅓ cup agave syrup, plus more for drizzling

⅓ cup plain coconut yogurt

1 8-ounce carton vanilla coconut yogurt

Vegan butter

You could bake this in a gluten-free pie crust too.

Blend the pumpkin, tofu, sugar, xanthan gum, syrup, and yogurt in a food processor until very smooth. Coat six 6-ounce heatproof ramekins with butter and fill with pumpkin mixture. Bake at 350 degrees for 30 minutes. Let cool. Run a butter knife blade around inside edges of ramekins and unmold puddings onto plates. Drizzle with agave syrup and dollop with vanilla yogurt. Makes 6 servings.

PAULA'S VERSION OF THE WORLD'S BEST GRANOLA

4 cups nuts of any kind

¼ cup coconut oil, melted

¼ cup agave syrup

¾ cup orange marmalade

¾ cup fruit-only apricot jam

1 cup filtered water

2 tablespoons high-quality vanilla extract

¼ teaspoon sea salt

8 cups gluten-free oats

Dried fruit, amount and type to taste

The truth about this recipe is that you don't have to restrict yourself to apricot jam, nor do you have to use marmalade, necessarily—so it's a good way to use up partial jars of jam or last year's canning efforts. But the marmalade, apricot and vanilla flavors are quite wonderful together.

Preheat oven to 225 degrees. Chop nuts in food processor. In a saucepan, make a liquid of coconut oil, agave, marmalade, jam, water, vanilla, and salt. Bring to a boil. Place nuts in a very large pan and pour liquid over them. Stir. Add oats and mix. Pay attention to dryness and add water to liquid mix if it looks like you are going to need it. But don't get it too wet.

Spread the mix evenly over two ungreased cookie sheets or as many as your oven will hold. Toast for one hour, and then begin checking every 20 minutes until granola is dark but not burning (in other words, slightly over-toast the mix). This may take several hours and varies completely from oven to oven. Stir in dried fruit after granola has cooled. Store well-sealed in a cool, dark place. Makes 32 ½-cup servings.

*Candied ginger, finely chopped, is also a good addition.

BANANA-PEACH CRUNCH

2 large organic bananas

1 ½ cups Paula's Version of the World's Best Granola

½ – ¾ cup vanilla coconut milk yogurt

½ cup canned coconut milk

1 ½ cups peaches, chopped (canned or fresh)

Extra vanilla coconut milk yogurt

Agave syrup

I dreamed this up as a dessert, actually, one night when we wanted something simple but sweet. It's the texture of the granola that carries this simple concoction and makes it a perfect centerpiece for breakfast.

Dice bananas and layer a portion of the bananas in a flat-bottomed, 24-ounce serving bowl. Drizzle with canned coconut milk and then top with a layer of granola. Continue layering in this fashion until ingredients are used up—you should have at least two layers but three is possible and preferable with the right bowl. Cover bowl with a towel and allow to set up in the fridge for an hour. Remove towel and top with peach slices and dabs of vanilla yogurt. Drizzle with agave syrup. Makes 2–4 servings.

SALADS AND SANDWICHES

I conducted an informal survey asking folks to tell me what they'd like to see in their favorite vegan and gluten-free recipe book. The most asked-for dish was salads, so I had to get to work, since we rarely wrote down any of our "frequent flyers."

WESTERN COLESLAW

¼ head green cabbage, very thinly sliced

¼ head red cabbage, very thinly sliced

2 carrots, chopped

½ green pepper, chopped

Vegenaise®

1 tablespoon agave syrup

2 teaspoons yellow mustard

1 teaspoon caraway seed

Sea salt to taste

Fresh cracked black pepper to taste

Paprika

The women in my family made the best coleslaw, but it was laden with cow's milk and sugar. I like my version just as well. The green pepper addition to this side dish is something I first noticed out West, where people simply call it "slaw."

Combine vegetables. Add Vegenaise® 1 tablespoon at a time until desired consistency is obtained. Add agave and mustard. Add caraway. Season to taste. Refrigerate for several hours or overnight. As a garnish, sprinkle with paprika before serving. Makes 6–8 servings.

DISAPPEARING KALE SLAW

½ pound kale, washed, stemmed, and finely chopped

¼ green cabbage head, finely chopped

¼ red cabbage head, finely chopped

4 green onions, thinly sliced

3 large carrots, grated

¾ cup hulled pumpkin seeds

2 large garlic cloves, minced

1 tablespoon fresh ginger, minced

2 tablespoons low-salt tamari

2 tablespoons canned coconut milk

1 cup Vegenaise®

This recipe was inspired by the Moscow (Idaho) Food Co-op's Famous Kale Slaw, which I buy almost every time I shop there. I love my version, but admittedly, I purposefully have not made theirs (even though the recipe is readily available) because to do so seems like a bit of sacrilege. If you've ever tried theirs, you know what I mean.

Mix vegetables in a large bowl. Place remaining ingredients, including pumpkin seeds, in blender and puree until smooth. Toss dressing with vegetables. Cover and refrigerate before serving. Makes 6–8 servings.

ENDIVE AND BOK CHOY IN CREAMY BASIL-GRAPEFRUIT VINAIGRETTE

DRESSING

1 large white grapefruit

8 fresh basil leaves

¼ cup extra-virgin olive oil

2 tablespoons white wine vinegar

2 tablespoons plain coconut milk yogurt

2 tablespoons honey

CANDIED GRAPEFRUIT

½ cup organic sugar

½ cup filtered water

SALAD

Curly endive

Curly bib lettuce

Baby bok choy

I was looking for a way to use the leftover endive and bok choy from East Meets West Burritos (see page 116) during the photo shoot. I was so surprised when this recipe ended up being good enough to include in the cookbook!

TO MAKE THE DRESSING: Remove grapefruit pulp from membrane, preserving as much juice and pulp as possible, and place in a small food processor. Set aside peel. Chop basil leaves finely and add to grapefruit pulp. Add remaining dressing ingredients and process until very smooth and creamy. Cover and refrigerate.

TO MAKE THE CANDIED GRAPEFRUIT: Cut half of a grapefruit peel into ¼" x 1" pieces. Bring sugar and water to a boil over medium heat. Boil peel pieces in sugar water until translucent. Remove with slotted spoon, allowing liquid to drain away. Set aside peel pieces on parchment paper to cool.

TO MAKE THE SALAD: Remove white stems from baby bok choy, slice crosswise into ¼" slices, and set aside. Tear endive and lettuce into bite-sized pieces and set aside. For each salad, arrange laying 3 bok choy leaves so that they protrude above the edge of a bowl or at cross positions on a salad plate. Arrange 2 large endive leaves and 2 large lettuce leaves on top of bok choy leaves. Arrange sliced bok choy stems on top of endive. Drizzle dressing on salad. Garnish with candied grapefruit. Serve immediately. Makes enough dressing to for 6–8 salads.

BUTTER-DILL SALAD

DRESSING

1 cup freshly-squeezed orange juice

¼ cup extra virgin olive oil

1 tablespoon white wine vinegar

2 tablespoons plain coconut milk yogurt

2 tablespoons agave syrup

1 teaspoon arrowroot powder

SALAD

1 large head butter lettuce

1 grapefruit, sectioned and sliced

1 bunch radishes, thinly sliced

½ cup fresh basil, chopped

2 tablespoons fresh dill, finely snipped

1 avocado, chopped

Several recipes in this book came about because I was trying to mimic something I'd eaten in a restaurant. Butter-Dill Salad was inspired by a lunch I enjoyed at a great restaurant called Fork in downtown Boise.

TO MAKE THE DRESSING: In a small saucepan over low heat, whisk together all dressing ingredients. Simmer on low until dressing starts to thicken. Remove from heat and allow to cool. Cover and refrigerate.

TO MAKE THE SALAD: Just before serving, tear lettuce into bite-sized chunks and place in a medium-sized serving bowl. Toss in radishes, basil, and dill. Add grapefruit and avocado and toss with dressing. Makes 4 generous servings.

MIGHTY FINE TACO SALAD

TOPPING

2 cups dried kidney beans

2 quarts + 1 ½ cups filtered water

1 cup uncooked basmati rice

2 tablespoons sunflower oil

½ large white onion, chopped

1 heaping tablespoon hot Italian oregano

2 tablespoons vegan butter

Fresh ground black pepper to taste

SALAD

1 head romaine lettuce, chopped

2 tomatoes, diced

1 leek, chopped

1 head red cabbage, chopped

1 cup grated vegan cheddar cheese

1 avocado, chopped

Cayenne pepper to taste

Medium salsa

Tortilla chips

This makes enough for company or leftovers, whichever comes first.

TO MAKE THE TOPPING: Soak beans overnight and drain. Cook on low in a slow cooker in 2 quarts filtered water for 9 hours. In a medium-sized pan, soak basmati in 1 ½ cups filtered water for 20 minutes. Place over medium heat and bring to a boil. Cook over very low heat, covered, for 20 minutes. Remove from heat and set aside, covered, until ready to use. In a large skillet, sauté onion in oil until caramelized. Add cooked beans and half the oregano and stir. Cook beans, partially covered and at a hard simmer, until half the juice is boiled off. Add butter. Top with the remaining oregano and lots of pepper. Simmer for 15 more minutes, cover completely, and turn off heat.

TO MAKE THE SALAD: Meanwhile, make a tossed salad of chopped romaine, tomato, leek, and red cabbage. You will need 2 cups of salad per serving. Arrange each salad on a dinner plate and top with cooked basmati. Sprinkle with cheese and chopped avocado. Spoon beans over the rice. Sprinkle with a few dashes of cayenne, and then top with salsa and crumbled tortilla chips. Makes enough beans and rice for 4 generous servings.

NEW KENTUCKY POTATO SALAD

3 pounds red potatoes

2 stalks celery, finely chopped

1 medium-sized yellow onion, finely chopped

¾ cup sweet pickle relish

1+ cups Vegenaise®

1+ tablespoons prepared mustard

Sea salt to taste

Fresh ground black pepper to taste

Paprika to taste

In *Blue Moon Vegetarian*, I make a bit of noise about my unwillingness to give up a certain brand of mayonnaise when making my mother's potato salad. Well, that was before I tried Vegenaise®.

Boil potatoes until they just barely yield to a fork. Do not overcook. Turn off heat, cover pan, and let potatoes sit in water until completely cool. This guarantees the potatoes will have the correct texture. In a large bowl, quarter potatoes lengthwise and then quarter again horizontally. Add celery, onion, and relish. Mix. Stir in 1 cup Vegenaise®, and then add 1 tablespoon at a time and stir until mixture is slightly creamy. Stir in 1 tablespoon mustard, and then add more to taste. Add salt and pepper to taste. Garnish liberally with paprika. Cover and refrigerate overnight before serving. Makes 6–8 servings.

SUNNY PASTA SALAD

DRESSING

Zest from 1 large orange (about 3 tablespoons)

½ cup unsweetened coconut milk beverage

2 tablespoons extra-virgin olive oil

¼ cup Vegenaise®

1 tablespoon prepared mustard

Juice from ½ medium-sized lemon

2 tablespoons coconut sugar

2 teaspoons fresh basil, very finely chopped

1 tablespoon dill, finely snipped

⅛ teaspoon sea salt

Pinch garlic granules

Pinch yellow cumin

Pinch white pepper

SALAD

1 box quinoa veggie curls pasta

1 medium-sized red bell pepper, finely chopped

1 stalk celery, very thinly sliced

2 green onions, finely snipped

½ cup hazelnuts, finely chopped

I've never liked pasta salad, likely for obvious reasons—those noodles were full of gluten. But once I figured out I needed to be gluten-free, for some reason I started craving a good pasta salad. Go figure. This one is a potluck prize.

TO MAKE THE DRESSING: Whisk dressing ingredients together in a medium-sized bowl. Cover and refrigerate.

TO MAKE THE SALAD: Cook quinoa pasta according to package directions. Allow to cool. Stir in vegetables. Add dressing and nuts. Cover and refrigerate overnight or for several hours. Makes 8 generous servings.

ALMOST NIRVANA FRUIT SALAD

1 cup huckleberries

2 bananas, sliced

1 nectarine, chopped

1 peach, chopped

1 12-ounce can pineapple chunks

1 cup walnut halves, coarsely chopped

2 tablespoons pineapple juice

2 teaspoons lemon juice

2 teaspoons lime juice

1 teaspoon agave syrup

½ cup sparkling mineral water

¼ cup candied ginger, finely chopped

2 tablespoons chocolate mint leaves, crushed*

1 ounce dark chocolate, grated (I like Green & Black's® Organic)

Honey

Gluten-free dark chocolate wafer cookies

This recipe appeared in *Blue Moon Vegetarian* and was inspired by my Grandma Hazel, who doused hers in 7-Up. Mostly, I think, it was a vehicle for those teensy little multi-colored marshmallows. The two things together, I'm certain, contributed to her development of diabetes. Trust me—you will not miss either ingredient. One word of caution: make this salad when no one is at home, just in case you want to eat the entire batch yourself.

Mix fruits and walnuts in a medium-sized bowl. Mix juices, agave syrup, and sparkling water, pour over fruit, and toss lightly with ginger and mint leaves. Separate into serving bowls, top with grated chocolate, and drizzle lightly with honey. Garnish with dark chocolate wafer cookies and serve immediately, or else the sauce loses its fizz. Makes 4 generous servings.

We grow our own chocolate mint. If you can't find it in stores, you can substitute regular mint leaves.

PHIL'S VEGETABLE ROLL-UPS

FILLING

1 12" carrot, grated

¼ cucumber, finely chopped

1 celery stalk, finely chopped

½ – 1 cup red cabbage, finely chopped

¼ cup Can't Be Cheese (see page 95)

½ cup walnuts, finely chopped

DRESSING

1 cup plain coconut milk yogurt

¼ cup Vegenaise®

2 tablespoons horseradish mustard

1 teaspoon hot pepper sauce (I like Louisiana Red)

ROLL UPS

Lettuce leaves

1 recipe Surprising Tortillas (see page 96) or purchased gluten-free tortillas

Picnics? Yes. Saturday lunches? Yes. Forgettable? No.

Mix the filling ingredients together in a medium-sized bowl. In a small bowl, combine the dressing ingredients. Add enough dressing to the vegetable mixture to moisten it. Spoon vegetable mixture into lettuce-lined tortillas and roll into burritos. Save any leftover dressing to thin with sunflower oil for a hot but yummy salad dressing. Makes 4–6 roll-ups.

SALADS AND SANDWICHES

HIPPIE EGG SALAD

1 14-ounce package extra-firm tofu, drained and pressed (see page 32)

½ medium-sized yellow onion, minced

¼ green pepper, minced

1 4-ounce jar capers

½ cup sweet pickle relish

2 tablespoons nutritional yeast

Vegenaise®

1 teaspoon prepared mustard

1 teaspoon agave syrup

Sea salt to taste

Fresh cracked black pepper to taste

Lettuce

Your choice of gluten-free bread

My introduction to tofu was at a hippie fair at Haight-Ashbury in San Francisco in the 1970s. It was love at first bite, but it was thirty years later that I first experimented with eggless egg salad.

Crumble tofu in a bowl and mix with vegetables and relish. Add Vegenaise® a tablespoon at a time until desired texture is reached. Add nutritional yeast, mustard, and agave. Add seasonings to taste. Refrigerate several hours or overnight. Stir before spooning between bread slices. Dress with lettuce leaves. Makes enough filling for 4–6 hearty sandwiches.

CHICK SALAD

2 cups cooked chickpeas, mashed

½ medium-sized yellow onion, finely chopped

2 celery ribs, chopped

¼ red pepper, finely minced

¼ cup sweet pickle relish

Vegenaise®

2 teaspoons miso

1 teaspoon prepared mustard

Sea salt to taste

Fresh cracked black pepper to taste

Lettuce

Your choice of gluten-free bread

This is, rather obviously, meant to fill that blank spot left by chicken and tuna salads, which, as with other things from the animal kingdom, I actually don't miss. But I am glad I decided to give this a try. Great lunch or road-trip fare.

In a medium-sized bowl, mix chickpeas with vegetables and relish. Blend miso, mustard, and a small amount of Vegenaise® together and add to vegetable mixture. Stir in Vegenaise® a tablespoon at a time until desired texture is reached. Add seasonings to taste. Process slightly in a food processor, leaving mixture coarse and somewhat chunky. Refrigerate several hours or overnight. Spoon between bread slices. Dress with lettuce leaves. Makes enough chick salad for 4–6 hearty sandwiches.

SPICY TLT ON TOAST

MARINATED TEMPEH

1 8-ounce package Tofurky® tempeh

2 tablespoons liquid smoke

1 tablespoon coconut aminos

1 tablespoon pure maple syrup

1 tablespoon filtered water

1 teaspoon smoked paprika

1 teaspoon alder smoked sea salt

1 tablespoon toasted sesame oil

DRESSING

2 tablespoons Vegenaise®

2 tablespoons miso

Hot sauce to taste (optional)

SANDWICH

Lettuce

Tomato slices

Your choice of gluten-free bread

I have Blue Scorcher in Astoria, Oregon, to thank for inspiring this one.

TO MAKE THE MARINATED TEMPEH: Slice tempeh lengthwise into the thinnest strips possible. In a small bowl, stir together liquid smoke, aminos, syrup, water, paprika, and salt until salt dissolves. In a small baking dish, arrange tempeh, pouring marinade between and around strips. Add a small amount of water if necessary to completely submerge tempeh. Marinate, covered, in the refrigerator overnight. Fry tempeh in oil until toasted around the edges.

TO MAKE THE DRESSING: Mix Vegenaise®, miso, and hot sauce.

TO MAKE THE SANDWICH: Toast bread, and then spread with miso dressing. Arrange tempeh on toast with tomato and lettuce. Makes enough tempeh for 2–3 sandwiches.

FIVE-BEAN SANDWICH SPREAD

FILLING

1 cup Five Beans (see page 109), drained, chilled, and mashed

2 tablespoons nutritional yeast

¼ cup chopped green pepper

2 tablespoons capers

2 tablespoons pimentos, finely chopped

2 tablespoons sweet pickle relish

2 tablespoons black olives, finely chopped

1 teaspoon orange zest

1+ tablespoons Vegenaise®

Sea salt to taste

Fresh cracked black pepper to taste

SANDWICH

Butter lettuce

Yellow tomato slices

Can't Be Cheese (see page 95)

Your choice of gluten-free bread

Obviously I'm big on sandwich fixings—likely from years and years of a busy writing life and being a mother reliant on cold cuts. I'm always looking for a quick way around mealtime, especially on weekends, so I can get back to work. Five Beans is a mix I stumbled on by accident: a "what's in the cupboard" phenomenon. The sandwich spread is one of those recipes that evolved over time, and, admittedly, it makes no sense whatsoever. How can it possibly taste as good as it tastes?

Process one cup of Five Beans in a food processor briefly and move to a medium-sized mixing bowl. Add nutritional yeast, green pepper, capers, pimentos, relish, olives, orange zest, and enough Vegenaise® to moisten the mixture. Season with salt and pepper. Spoon onto bread slices. Dress with butter lettuce, tomato, and Can't Be Cheese. Makes enough sandwich spread for 2 hearty sandwiches.

SOUP KETTLE

One reason I know I won't ever go for a 100% raw diet is that I can't give up soups. They are too much a part of my mountain heritage, too much a thing of comfort, and too much a symbol of the resourcefulness I learned as a young mother—a way to use up the bits and dabs of food inherent to a busy kitchen. This collection of favorites is the result of a lifetime of playing with those bits and dabs.

CHARD SUMMER SOUP

3 tablespoons vegan butter

3 tablespoons white rice flour

3 cups vegetable broth

1 green tomato, very finely chopped*

1 leek, very finely sliced

2 bunches chard, chopped

¼ cup mint, chopped, plus more for garnish

Filtered water

4 strawberries, sliced

People look at me sideways when I talk about how much I love cold soups. I just think there is nothing more refreshing on a hot summer day.

Make a roux by melting butter and gradually stirring in rice flour over medium-low heat. Add broth, stirring in a bit at a time to avoid lumps. Add vegetables and mint. Cook over low heat until vegetables are very soft, adding small amounts of water as needed to keep mixture thinned. Remove from heat and allow to cool. Puree in blender. Garnish with mint leaves and strawberry slices. Serve cold. Makes 2 servings.

*If green tomatoes are not available, tomatillos make an acceptable substitute.

GARDEN LENTIL SOUP

- 1 cup dried French green lentils
- ½ cup dried baby brown lentils
- 1 cup diced white onion
- 5 cloves garlic, minced
- 4 quarts filtered water
- 3 carrots, cut into ¼" coins
- 2 cups bok choy, chopped
- Sea salt to taste
- Fresh ground black pepper to taste
- Tony Chachere's® Original Creole Seasoning to taste

This is one of my favorite recipes from *Blue Moon Vegetarian*.

Add first five ingredients to a pot and bring to full boil. Simmer for 1 hour or until lentils are soft. Add carrots. Cook 10 minutes or until carrots are partially soft. Add bok choy and simmer 2–3 minutes. Add creole seasoning, pepper and salt to taste. Makes 6 generous servings.

GREAT (E)SCAPE VICHYSSOISE

- 3 tablespoons vegan butter
- 3 tablespoons chickpea flour
- 3 cups vegetable broth
- 1 medium-sized red potato, peeled and chopped
- 2 thick bunches scapes, finely chopped
- Sea salt to taste
- Paprika to taste

Scapes are those curly things that arise out of the top of garlic. They are available in our area in July and disappear quickly from our local food co-op. For some reason, the garlic in our garden doesn't quite produce them. Whatever it takes to acquire them, they are worth the effort: great on salads but unforgettable in this chilled soup.

Make a roux by melting butter and slowly stirring in flour over low heat. Stir in broth a few tablespoons at a time to avoid lumps. Add potato and scapes, leaving a few scapes for garnish. Cook over low heat until potatoes are very, very soft, about 45 minutes, adding small amounts of additional broth as needed to keep mixture thinned. Allow to cool. Puree in blender. Salt to taste. Garnish with finely chopped raw scapes and a dash of paprika, and serve cold with grilled vegan cheese triangles and watermelon wedges. Makes 3–4 servings.

SPICY CHILI BEAN STEW

2 cups dried red beans

4 quarts filtered water

¼ cup sunflower oil

1 large red onion

6 cloves garlic

1 red bell pepper

¼ cup dried celery leaves, crushed

1 teaspoon dried basil

1 teaspoon fresh ground black pepper

2 teaspoons cumin

2 tablespoons paprika

2 tablespoons chili powder

½ teaspoon cayenne

½ teaspoon ground coriander

¼ teaspoon crushed chipotle chili peppers

1 tablespoon agave syrup

2 squares very dark chocolate

2 28-ounce cans Muir Glen® Organic Chopped Fire-Roasted Tomatoes

1 15-ounce can tomato sauce

½ cup hulled hemp seed

Vegetable broth

Sea salt to taste

Vegan cheddar cheese, shredded

Plain coconut milk yogurt

We made this heartwarming stew and carted it to book signings when we were promoting *Blue Moon Vegetarian*. It's soulful and perfect for a snowy Sunday evening.

Combine beans and 2 quarts of water in a large soup pot. Bring to a boil. Remove from heat and allow to cool. Drain. Return beans to pot and add the last 2 quarts of water. Bring to boil. Lower heat and cook uncovered until beans are soft, approximately 2 hours, and then set aside. In a separate skillet, sauté onion, garlic, and bell pepper in oil until just starting to soften. Stir in all spices and herbs except hemp seed, agave syrup, and chocolate.

Add vegetable mixture to beans, along with tomatoes and tomato sauce, using vegetable broth to thin as necessary. Allow to simmer for 30 minutes or so, and then sample. Adjust spice and seasoning to taste. Add hemp seed. Simmer on low another 30 minutes—do not allow to boil. Allow stew to rest and cool before serving. Top with a bit of shredded cheese and yogurt. Serve with a handful of crushed tortilla chips. Makes 8–12 hearty servings.

HERBED FRENCH LENTIL SOUP

¼ cup extra-virgin olive oil

2 red onions, finely chopped

2 carrots, grated

6 cloves garlic, coarsely chopped

2 bay leaves

¼ cup dried parsley

1 teaspoon ground rosemary

1 teaspoon dried basil

1 teaspoon fresh ground black pepper

1 teaspoon sea salt

Dash of cayenne

4 cups vegetable broth

2 cups dried organic French green lentils

8 cups filtered water

We live just down the hill from the lentil capital of the world, so we have many, many different kinds of lentils available to us. People frequently ask if the type of lentil you use really matters, and the answer is that yes, it does. The flavors and textures of lentils can vary considerably.

Sauté onion, carrots, and garlic in olive oil in a soup kettle until onion is transparent. Add spices. Add broth and lentils. Add water. Bring to boil. Simmer uncovered over low heat for 1 hour or until lentils are soft. Serve with gluten-free pita wedges and hummus or homemade Can't Be Cheese (see page 95). Makes 4-6 servings.

BABY LENTIL STEW

2 cups dried baby brown lentils

4 red potatoes, cubed

4 stalks celery, chopped

1 large white (not yellow) onion, chopped

4 carrots, chopped

4 cloves garlic, chopped

1 8-ounce can tomato paste

2 bay leaves

2 teaspoons thyme

1 – 2 quarts vegetable broth

2 tablespoons coconut aminos

Sea salt to taste

Fresh ground black pepper to taste

Lentils cook quickly and do well in a slow cooker, so they are perfect for busy days and when you simply don't feel like spending too much time in the kitchen. This recipe also freezes nicely.

Rinse lentils and cover in a kettle with boiling water. Cook over low heat until lentils begin to soften but leave firm. Drain and add potatoes, celery, onion, carrots, garlic, tomato paste, bay leaves, and thyme. Add enough broth to cover ingredients. Bring to a boil. Cover and simmer until vegetables reach desired firmness. Remove bay leaves. Season with coconut aminos. Then add pepper and salt to taste. Allow to rest uncovered for 15 minutes before serving. Makes 6–8 servings.

TWO-BEAN CURRIED BISQUE

2 cups leftover cooked pinto beans

2 cups leftover cooked navy beans

2 cups vegetable broth

1 medium-sized onion, coarsely chopped

4 cloves garlic

2 tablespoons toasted sesame oil

2 tablespoons miso

2 tablespoons tahini

2 teaspoons coconut sugar

2 teaspoons thyme

2 teaspoons basil leaf

2 teaspoons yellow curry powder

1 teaspoons garlic granules

1 teaspoons coriander

1 teaspoons white pepper

1 teaspoon fresh cracked black pepper

1 teaspoons alder smoked sea salt

Cilantro

Lemon zest

You've probably noticed that a number of recipes in this book include mixed beans and ask for beans that have already been cooked instead of instructing you to cook them. The reason is simple: flavor and texture. Fresh-cooked beans do not taste or behave the same in recipes as beans that have rested in the freezer or refrigerator for a while. Canned beans, well, canned beans are a waste of money, and they are quite inferior when compared to home-cooked. Regardless, it's the slow-cooking that makes this soup rich and decadent.

Puree all ingredients except cilantro and lemon zest in a blender. Simmer in slow cooker on low 6–8 hours. Garnish with cilantro and lemon zest. Makes 8 servings.

EXOTIC BLACK-EYED CHILI

4 cups dried black-eyed peas

4 quarts filtered water plus extra for soaking

2 dried serrano peppers

8 cloves fresh garlic

1 large onion, finely chopped

1 stalk celery, finely chopped

2 tablespoons medium chili powder

2 tablespoons smoked paprika

2 teaspoons cumin powder

1 teaspoon ground coriander

1 teaspoon dried basil leaves, finely crumbled

1 teaspoon rosemary leaves, ground with mortar and pestle

1 teaspoon oregano

1 teaspoon mustard

1 tablespoon peanut butter

2 ounces very dark chocolate

1 tablespoon coconut oil

2 15-ounce cans Kirkland Signature™ Organic Stewed Tomatoes

Sea salt to taste

Phil and our dinner guest looked at me sideways when I served this the first time. The cinnamon and curry leaves it originally contained completely overwhelmed the confluence of milder flavors. This version—well, this version gets it right.

Cover beans with water in a large pot and bring to boil. Turn off heat and soak until cool. Drain. In the same pot, add 4 quarts filtered water and add beans, vegetables, spices, and herbs, and then simmer over medium heat until beans are soft. Remove chili pods. Add remaining ingredients. Continue to simmer on very low heat for 1 hour or transfer to a slow cooker on low and cook for several hours. Add sea salt to taste. Serve with cornbread. Makes 8–12 servings.

ICEBOX SOUP

2 cups leftover noodles and/or rice

2 cups leftover veggies

1 cup Five Beans (see page 109)

1 28-ounce can Muir Glen® Organic Diced Fire Roasted Tomatoes

2 cups vegetable broth

2 tablespoons extra-virgin olive oil

2 tablespoons vegan butter

2 teaspoons garlic granules

1 teaspoon tarragon

1 teaspoon dried basil

¼ cup dried parsley

2 teaspoons smoked paprika

¼ cup hulled hemp seed

¼ cup pine nuts

⅛ teaspoon crushed chipotle chili peppers

Filtered water

Sea salt to taste

Fresh ground black pepper to taste

Tony Chachere's® Original Creole Seasoning to taste

Yes, I love thinking of ways to use up leftovers and like to freeze small amounts of leftover everything, just so I can occasionally make this soup.

Combine all ingredients except salt, pepper, and creole seasoning in a large kettle. Add as much water as needed to thin soup. Bring to boil on high heat, stirring frequently. Immediately lower temperature and simmer on very low heat, covered, stirring occasionally, for 3–4 hours, or use a slow cooker on low for eight hours. Add salt, creole seasoning, and liberal amounts of pepper just before serving. Makes 6–8 servings.

Chocolate Chai Smoothie
(page 36)

Toasted coconut mocha frappuccino
(page 37)

Day at the Beach
(page 39)

Blue Moon Biscuits and Gravy
(page 43)

Skillet Cakes
(page 47)

Paula's Version of the World's Best Granola

(page 51)

Endive and Bok Choy in Creamy Basil-Grapefruit Vinaigrette

(page 55)

New Kentucky Potato Salad
(page 58)

Sunny Pasta Salad
(page 59)

Almost Nirvana Fruit Salad
(page 60)

Phil's Vegetable Roll-ups
(page 61)

Baby Lentil Stew
(page 71)

Grandma's 21st Century Panbread
(page 97)

Grilled Vegetable Polou
(page 99)

Phil's Infamous Baked Beans
(page 100)

Gingery Rice

(page 101)

Hot Tomato-Basil Casserole

(page 103)

Tomato Sauce
(page 106)

Everyday Grilling Burgers and Suzi's Home Fries
(page 122 and page 107)

**Phil's Hot and Spicy
Stir-Fried Green Beans**
(page 107)

Spring Fever
(page 108)

Phil's Fabulous Three-Bean Nachos

(page 112)

Phil's West Texas Greek Company Supper

(page 114)

East Meets West Burritos

(page 116)

Paula's Lasagna al Forno

(page 117)

Red-Hot Four-Star Two-Bean Burritos

(page 121)

White Sandwich Bread

(page 129)

Honey Oat Sandwich Bread
(page 130)

Orange Zucchini Muffins
(page 138)

Chocolate Cake Muffins

(page 140)

"Graham" Crackers

(page 143)

Coconut Macaroons
(page 144)

Peanut Butter Cookies
(page 145)

Chocolate Chip Cookies
(page 146)

Cherry Power Balls
(page 148)

International Day of Happiness Cookies
(page 151)

ON THE SIDE

On the Side *is not the same as being on the sidelines. These recipes are more than accessories. They complement main dishes by presenting intersecting flavors and textures and are nutrient powerhouses to boot.*

CAN'T BE CHEESE

2 cups cashews

4 cups filtered water

½ cup filtered water, chilled

½ cup full-fat canned coconut milk

3 probiotic capsules*

⅛ cup nutritional yeast

1 teaspoon sea salt

Juice from 1 lemon

A year ago I would have sworn I had left cheese behind. Then I started writing this cookbook and wanted to recommend something besides processed vegan "cheese" for certain recipes. I began working on the idea of a cheese made from nut milk and seriously thought I had invented something new. After a bit of investigating, I discovered a world of nut cheeses—even hard, aged ones. My version still remains different from most others, in that it also contains full-fat coconut milk. The flavor and creaminess makes me wonder why anyone ever started making cheese from cow's milk. Technically, I can't testify 100 percent to the "keeps indefinitely" part that other nut cheese recipes claim. My guess is that it won't last more than a couple of weeks—or as long as it takes the average family to eat a pound of cheese.

Soak cashews in 4 cups filtered water for 6 hours. Drain. Process in food processor with chilled water and coconut milk for 5 minutes or until completely smooth. Break open probiotic capsules and sprinkle over surface of mixture. Process for one minute. Add lemon juice, nutritional yeast, and salt and continue processing until smooth and creamy.

From this point on, wear latex gloves when working with cheese to prevent transmission of mold spores.

Prepare a 1-quart mesh strainer by lining it with several layers of cheesecloth, then set strainer in a colander with a plate or tray underneath the colander. Pour cashew mixture into cheesecloth, cover the entire system with a towel, and allow it to drain for 24 hours or until dripping has ceased.

Next, bring opposing corners of cheesecloth together and tie closed as tightly as possible with string. Move bundle to a clean glass bowl (not plastic), cover with a towel, and allow to rest on top of the refrigerator for 1 day (for a milder cheese) or 2 days (for sharper flavor). (Be prepared for the smell of working cheese in your house.) Serve right away or store in an airtight glass container (not plastic) and continue aging in the refrigerator. Makes approximately 1 pound of soft cheese.

Probiotic capsules are available at health food stores. If you've ever taken an antibiotic, your doctor has likely suggested you take a probiotic, too, to restore friendly microflora. In the kitchen, in addition to enhancing vegan cheeses, they can be used to start yogurt and kefir cultures. We keep them on hand for fighting viruses and intestinal upset. My favorite brand is Solaray Multidophilus™ 12.

SURPRISING TORTILLAS

92 grams chickpea flour

148 grams white rice flour

2 tablespoons room temperature coconut oil

1 teaspoon xanthan gum

1 teaspoon baking powder

2 teaspoons organic cane sugar

1 teaspoon salt

1 cup very warm filtered water

Extra-virgin olive oil

I did surprise myself with these yummy tortillas. Perfect for Phil's Vegetable Roll-Ups (see page 61) and East-Meets-West Burritos (see page 116).

Add the dry ingredients to a large mixing bowl and mix thoroughly. Add the cup of warm water to the bowl and mix the dry ingredients into the water by hand until you have an even mixture. Separate dough into six pieces and roll each piece into a ball. Place all but one of the dough balls back into the bowl and cover with plastic wrap until you're ready to work with them.

Between pieces of parchment paper, roll dough ball with rolling pin into a roughly circular shape and make as thin as possible—around ⅛" thick. Throw the tortilla onto a hot griddle (I recommend using a cast iron griddle on medium heat with just a smidge of olive oil) and let it cook approximately 1–2 minutes or until it puffs up and the bottom side develops brown spots. Flip the tortilla and cook the other side until is spotted as well.

Place cooked tortilla in a towel to stay warm and repeat steps with each dough ball until you've cooked all the tortillas. Roll one tortilla out while another is cooking, so that there is always a tortilla on the griddle. Serve warm. Makes 6 tortillas.

GRANDMA'S 21ST CENTURY PANBREAD

2 flax eggs (see page 24)

6 handfuls cornmeal

6 handfuls chickpea flour

1 handful white rice flour

3 tilts of the sunflower oil bottle

2 large* dollops plain coconut yogurt

3 large* pinches sea salt

3 large pinches baking powder

2 large pinches baking soda

2 large pinches xanthan gum

3 large dollops honey

1 cup unsweetened coconut milk beverage

Coconut oil

Sparkling mineral water

If I tell the truth, I don't normally measure what I put into recipes—except, of course, those created for this book. My grandmothers didn't either, nor my mother. We "feel" our way through. Here is an attempt at helping you learn how to trust your own intuition.

Preheat oven to 325 degrees. Prepare cast iron skillet by coating with a thin layer of coconut oil. Mix all ingredients in a large bowl. Do not over-stir and do not beat. Pour mixture into prepared cast iron skillet. Bake until toothpick comes out clean and bread pulls from the side of pan, 45–60 minutes. Allow to cool to room temperature. Serve with vegan butter and honey. Makes 8–12 servings.

A large pinch uses 3 fingers; a large dollop is an overloaded large cutlery spoon.

MOST HONORABLE HUMMUS

1 ½ cups dry chickpeas

¾ cup tahini

1 small onion, coarsely chopped

4 cloves garlic

1 teaspoon sea salt

2 tablespoons low-sodium tamari

2 tablespoons balsamic vinegar

2 tablespoons filtered water

1 tablespoon sesame oil

⅛ teaspoon red jalapeño sauce

Fresh cracked black pepper to taste

Fortunately, hummus is one of my favorite things, since often in restaurants it's the only fare on the menu that is both vegan and gluten-free. But even then I have to come to terms with the fact that it is likely neither homemade nor organic. I routinely have hummus for breakfast, since I like starting the day with a dose of protein. This recipe originated from a favorite and formative cookbook—*Moosewood Cookbook*—but has been tweaked to the point that the only remaining original ingredient is chickpeas. Recently, craving hummus but having no lemons on hand, I substituted balsamic vinegar, which created richness and depth I didn't know was missing. New rule at our house? No more lemon juice in the hummus.

Soak chickpeas overnight. Drain, cover with water, bring to a boil, and then lower heat to simmer. Cook until soft. Drain and allow to cool. Add all ingredients except pepper in food processor and process until a very smooth paste forms. Add pepper to taste. Allow to set several hours in the refrigerator or overnight. Serve with crudité or gluten-free crackers or use as a sandwich spread. Store in the refrigerator for up to a week. Makes approximately 4 cups.

GRILLED VEGETABLE POLOU

2 ½ cups vegetable broth

1 cup uncooked brown basmati rice

½ teaspoon ground ginger

1 large Walla Walla sweet onion

1 large green pepper

1 small eggplant

2 ripe medium-sized tomatoes or 12 cherry tomatoes

4 tablespoons extra-virgin olive oil

4 tablespoons sesame oil

2 tablespoons Trader Joe's® Organic Red Wine and Olive Oil Vinaigrette

2 tablespoons agave syrup

Pinch Tony Chachere's® Original Creole Seasoning

Pinch garlic granules

This is a favorite from *Blue Moon Vegetarian*, with a few adaptations; namely, I increased the amount of sauce, because there simply wasn't enough.

Bring vegetable broth to a boil in a medium-sized saucepan and add rice and ginger. Bring to a boil again, cover, and reduce heat to lowest setting. Simmer for 50 minutes. Remove from heat and allow to sit undisturbed for 30 minutes. Meanwhile, cube and skewer vegetables. Whisk together remaining ingredients, and brush onto kebobs. Grill until edges of vegetables are brown, turning as needed. Remove from skewer and arrange on a bed of rice. Drizzle with remaining basting sauce. Makes 4 servings.

PHIL'S INFAMOUS BAKED BEANS
(formerly Phil's Famous Baked Beans)

1 ½ cups leftover cooked great northern beans

1 ½ cups leftover cooked kidney beans

1 ½ cups leftover cooked black beans

1 medium-sized yellow onion, coarsely chopped

½ green pepper, coarsely chopped

½ cup vegetable broth*

⅓ cup ketchup

⅓ cup coconut sugar

1 tablespoon prepared mustard

1 tablespoon apple cider vinegar

1 teaspoon oregano

1 teaspoon cumin

1 teaspoon garlic granules

1 teaspoon alder smoked sea salt

1 teaspoon arrowroot

⅛ teaspoon fresh ground black pepper

⅛ teaspoon cayenne

This recipe came through Phil's family from California by way of Montana and originally used canned beans. I think it is silly and goofy to pay money for canned beans but admit to using them in my earlier years. They are a great convenience, but the flavor and texture are inferior, and they are ten times more expensive than cooking in batches and freezing your own. This recipe challenges you to do just that.

Preheat oven to 275 degrees. Mix beans together in an oven-safe casserole dish. Mince yellow onion and green pepper in a food processor. Add broth, ketchup, sugar, mustard, vinegar, and seasonings, and then process briefly to blend. Pour mixture over beans and blend thoroughly. Bake for 1 ½–2 hours or until sauce is very thick. You can also cook the beans in a slow cooker: cook for 6–8 hours on low or 3–4 hours on high. Makes 8–12 servings.

*If using canned beans, bean liquid may be substituted for broth.

GINGERY RICE
(Formerly Eggless in Clarkston)

1 tablespoon olive oil

3 garlic cloves, finely chopped

1 stalk celery, thinly sliced

⅓ red bell pepper, chopped

½ leek, thinly sliced

1 1" piece ginger root, peeled and minced

1 cup cooked brown basmati rice

1 cup cooked white basmati rice

1 tablespoon tamari sauce

Crushed chipotle chili pepper to taste

White pepper to taste

Just a basic rice dish, but yummy all the same. The name only made sense in the context of *Blue Moon Vegetarian*, so I changed it.

Heat oil, garlic, and celery over medium-high heat until celery just starts to soften. Add bell pepper, leek, and ginger. Stir fry until bell pepper is tender but still slightly crisp. Add rice and tamari. Season with chili pepper and white pepper to taste. Makes 4 servings.

SWEET LENTIL POLOU

1 tablespoon extra-virgin olive oil

1 small red onion, finely chopped

1 bay leaf

1 cup leftover or cooked brown basmati rice

1 tablespoon tomato paste

3 cups vegetable broth

¼ teaspoon cinnamon

Pinch cardamom

1 cup dried baby brown lentils

½ teaspoon sea salt

¼ teaspoon white pepper

½ cup dried currants

½ cup pine nuts

Very hot filtered water

This is another dish inspired by *Laurel's Kitchen* and a long-time favorite.

Preheat oven to 325 degrees. Sauté onion and bay leaf in olive oil over medium heat until onion is soft. Discard bay leaf. Add rice and stir until hot throughout. In a small bowl, mix tomato paste, broth, cinnamon, and cardamom. Add mixture to rice along with the lentils. Bring to a boil, cover, and simmer on very low heat for 30 minutes. Stir in salt and white pepper, fruit, and nuts. Pour mixture into casserole dish. Add very hot (not boiling) water as necessary to create a thick soup. Cover and bake 20–30 minutes. Serve with salad or vegetable raita. Makes 4 generous servings.

HOT TOMATO-BASIL CASSEROLE

2 cups filtered water

1 cup uncooked brown basmati rice

2 pounds fresh tomatoes, chopped

5 cloves garlic, minced

½ cup fresh basil, chopped

1 Walla Walla sweet onion, chopped

1 yellow squash, chopped

Fresh ground black pepper to taste

Tony Chachere's® Original Creole Seasoning to taste

1 dozen gluten-free saltines

Sometimes the simplest dishes are the most delectable, and that is certainly the case here. This one is perfect when paired with grilled tempeh.

Preheat oven to 350 degrees. Heat water to boiling. Add rice. Cover and cook on very low heat for 45 minutes. Meanwhile, stew tomatoes, garlic, basil, and onion, adding water as necessary to maintain a medium-consistency sauce. Simmer covered on very low heat for 20 minutes. Add squash. Season with pepper and creole seasoning to taste. Alternate layers of rice and tomato mixture with layers of crumbled saltines at least twice in a baking dish. Bake for 20 minutes. Allow to rest 10 minutes and serve. Makes 4—6 servings.

FETTUCCINE CAULIFREDO

6 heaping cups cauliflower florets (equivalent of 1 large head of cauliflower)

1 tablespoon sunflower oil

4 – 5 large cloves garlic, sliced

½ – 1 cup canned coconut milk

6 tablespoons nutritional yeast

1 tablespoon prepared mustard

2 tablespoons vegan butter

¼ large onion, chopped

1 teaspoon fine grain sea salt

½ teaspoon white pepper

1 package gluten-free fettuccine or pasta of choice

Fresh parsley, chopped

Fresh ground black pepper

My favorite food website is www.OhSheGlows.com. I won't go so far as to say that I wish I had Angela Liddon's gift for cooking, but I'm certainly glad she is on the planet at the same time as I am, so that I can avail myself of all the wonderful recipes she dreams up. I literally have visions of her peanut butter cups and swear if you try one you'll never buy packaged ones again. The following recipe is inspired by her Alfredo sauce, but I've morphed it so many times that the only thing the two dishes have in common is perhaps the cauliflower.

Steam cauliflower over medium heat until very tender and allow to cool slightly. Meanwhile, add oil to skillet and sauté onion and garlic over very low heat for 5–6 minutes or until quite brown. In high speed blender, puree cooked and drained cauliflower, sautéed garlic and onion, milk, nutritional yeast, mustard, salt, and white pepper. Blend until smooth sauce forms. Stop and use a tamper stick as needed. Pour into saucepan and heat thoroughly over low heat. Add vegan butter at this point if desired. Cook fettuccine according to package instructions and drain. Return to pan and stir in sauce, reheating as necessary. Garnish with chopped parsley and black pepper. Makes 4–6 servings.

SQUASH BLOSSOMS IN CASHEW CREAM

2 cups cashews

3 cups + 1 ½ cups filtered water

¼ cup nutritional yeast

Juice from 1 lemon

½ teaspoon sea salt

1 capsule multi-strain probiotic*

8 cups fresh squash blossoms

2 tablespoons vegan butter

1 12-ounce box gluten-free linguini

Smoked Hungarian paprika

Squash Blossoms are like garlic scapes: they only come around once a year, so when they do, be sure to nab some at your local farmers market or harvest from your own plants to "thin the herd." This decadent side dish will wow guests and make hesitant children into converts. The probiotic starts a fermentation process that gives the cream a slightly sour flavor, like a mild sour cream. Slices of lily melon—a variety of Crenshaw—complement these flavors and are a perfect accompaniment.

Soak cashews in 3 cups water for 6 hours. Drain. Process in high-powered blender or food processor with 1 ½ cups water for 5 minutes until completely smooth. Add lemon juice, nutritional yeast, and salt and continue processing until smooth and creamy. Break open probiotic capsule and sprinkle over mixture. Pulse several times to blend. Move to a clean glass bowl or dish, cover and allow to sit at room temperature for 4–6 hours.

Just before serving, cook linguini according to package directions. Meanwhile, sauté squash blossoms in butter over low heat for 10 minutes or until limp. Drain excess liquid. Return to pan and add cashew cream. Heat thoroughly over low heat. **Do not simmer or boil.** Remove from heat and serve over pasta. Sprinkle with paprika. You may also choose to serve this dish cold. Makes 4–6 servings.

*Probiotic capsules are available at health food stores. If you've ever taken an antibiotic, your doctor has likely suggested you take a probiotic, too, to restore friendly microflora. In the kitchen, in addition to enhancing vegan cheeses, they can be used to start yogurt and kefir cultures. We keep them on hand for fighting viruses and intestinal upset. My favorite brand is Solaray Multidophilus™ 12.

TOMATO SAUCE

¼ cup extra-virgin olive oil

2 medium red onions, chopped

4 cloves garlic, mashed

1 bell pepper, chopped

3 fresh bay leaves

2 tablespoons fresh oregano

1 tablespoon fresh thyme

1 tablespoon fresh basil

2 teaspoons fresh rosemary

2 teaspoons fennel seed

½ cup fresh parsley

2 tablespoons paprika

3 carrots, grated

6 cups chopped fresh tomatoes

2 6-ounce cans tomato paste

1 teaspoon fresh ground pepper

¼ teaspoon dried red chili seeds

2 tablespoons agave syrup

Vegetable broth

I have made this sauce a thousand times and have canned hundreds of quarts of it. When my children were growing up, it was the only tomato sauce I ever used. The very flavor of it brings up a bushel of memories.

Sauté onion, garlic, and pepper in olive oil until onion is transparent. Toss herbs in a dry pan over medium heat until crumbly. Stir herbs and carrots into onion mix. Add tomatoes, paste, and seasonings. Thin with broth as needed. Cover and simmer for 20–30 minutes. For optimum flavor, store sauce in the refrigerator for 24 hours before using. Ladle over corn macaroni. Makes 8–10 servings.

SUZI'S BAKED HOME FRIES

2 large Russet potatoes

Extra-virgin olive oil

Sea salt to taste

I did not expect my photographer to be a contributor to this cookbook, but when she wanted fries to photograph with the Everyday Grilling Burgers (see page 122) and told me about how she bakes them, I begged her to let me include her recipe. They are so yummy and certifiable comfort food—and they'll keep you from missing deep-fried French fries, which are triglyceride-raising demons.

Preheat oven to 450 degrees. Line cookie sheet with foil and spread with a thin layer of olive oil. Cut potatoes into long fries ½" square and rinse in cold water. Soak fries in ice water for 10 minutes. Dry between paper towels. Place on prepared foil and drizzle with olive oil. Toss to coat evenly. Sprinkle with sea salt. Bake 15 minutes on each side until golden brown. Allow to cool slightly before serving. Makes 2 servings.

PHIL'S HOT AND SPICY STIR-FRIED GREEN BEANS

¼ cup filtered water

1 pound frozen Kirkland Signature™ Organic Green Beans

2 tablespoons sunflower oil

Garlic granules to taste

Sea salt to taste

Fresh ground black pepper to taste

Tony Chachere's® Original Creole Seasoning to taste

If these are prepared correctly, the seasonings become little crunchy chunks of yumminess.

Heat water in wok or round-bottomed skillet over medium heat until very hot. Add frozen beans and cook until water evaporates. Meanwhile, heat oil in a separate skillet. Sieve beans and drop into heated oil, stirring until evenly coated. Cook on medium-high heat, stirring occasionally, for 10 minutes or until edges of beans start to brown and crisp. Add liberal amounts of seasoning and stir. Once seasonings form clumps, remove skillet from heat. Allow beans to cool slightly before serving. Makes 3–4 servings.

ON THE SIDE

SPRING FEVER

2 cups uncooked brown basmati rice

4 cups filtered water

1 tablespoon olive oil

1 medium-sized zucchini, halved and cut into 1" pieces

1 pound asparagus, cut into 1" pieces

2 tablespoons sunflower oil

⅓ cup yellow onion, chopped

1 1" piece ginger root, peeled and minced

1 red bell pepper, cut into 1" pieces

1 cup red cabbage, chopped

1 teaspoon crushed red pepper

½ teaspoon fresh ground black pepper

1 teaspoon garlic granules

1 tablespoon Trader Ming's Soyaki

Tony Chachere's® Original Creole Seasoning to taste

Roasted cashews

I don't mean to promote certain stores or brands, but when I do mention them, it's because it's the brand that makes the recipe turn out best—not because the book has been sponsored in any way. In this instance, Trader Ming's Soyaki from Trader Joe's® makes this recipe one of our favorite stir-fries. We love to make it when the first crop of asparagus arrives. It's like a promise of easier days ahead.

Bring water and olive oil to a boil in a medium-sized saucepan. Add rice, and then lower heat and cover. Simmer for 45 minutes or until done. (Rice may be cooked ahead of time and refrigerated until needed.) Steam asparagus pieces until still crunchy but not raw, and then set aside.

Heat sunflower oil in a large wok or round-bottomed skillet over medium-high heat until extremely hot. Add onion, ginger, and red bell pepper and cook, stirring constantly, until translucent. Add asparagus, zucchini, and cabbage, stirring constantly, until cabbage and asparagus become bright in color. Stir in crushed red pepper, black pepper, and garlic. Add rice and stir. Add Soyaki, and then season to taste with creole seasoning. Top each portion with a handful of roasted cashews. Makes 6 generous servings.

CENTER STAGE

This section is all about hearty main dishes, including some that are designed to make use of leftovers. As always, feel free to experiment and make them your own.

FIVE BEANS

1 cup each dried kidney beans, navy beans, black beans, small red beans, and yellow lentils

1 large yellow onion, chopped

1 head garlic, peeled and minced

I like having batches of Five Beans on hand in the freezer in quart-sized containers (I usually use canning jars). You can make them the central component of a meal by warming them and heaping them on a bed of brown rice or millet with steamed veggies on the side; mashing them into Five Bean Sandwich Spread (see page 65); using them to make burgers; adding some chili powder and plopping them on a bed of mixed greens topped with avocado and tomato (see In-a-Pinch Bean Bowl on page 126); or using them as the basis for Icebox Soup (see page 74). A soup kettle of possibilities.

Rinse beans and lentils and place in a large stew pot. Cover with water and bring to boil. Turn off heat and let sit 1 hour. Add onion, garlic, and enough water that the liquid covering the beans is several inches deep. Simmer on low 1–2 hours or until beans are soft. Divide and store in freezer or refrigerator. Makes 5–6 quarts or 20–24 1-cup servings.

NUTTY BLACK BEAN BURGERS

3 flax eggs (see page 24)

½ cup onion, diced

½ tablespoon sunflower oil

1 large garlic clove, minced

2 teaspoons xanthan gum

1 cup gluten-free oats, ground into flour

1 ½ cups gluten-free bread crumbs

1 cup grated carrots

1 cup leftover cooked black beans, mashed

¼ cup finely chopped fresh cilantro

⅓ cup almonds, ground into meal

½ cup sunflower seeds, ground into meal

1 tablespoon coconut oil

1 tablespoon tamari

1 ½ teaspoon chili powder

1 teaspoon cumin

1 teaspoon oregano

½ teaspoon sea salt

Coconut oil

Fresh ground black pepper to taste

This book contains four types of burgers. I can't seem to help myself. Every time we want to grill, I make something new from whatever ingredients we have on hand. This one is likely the most complicated and makes good use of leftovers, but it also freezes very well, so don't be afraid to double the batch.

Prepare flax eggs and set aside. In large skillet, sauté onions and garlic in oil. Place in a large mixing bowl with all remaining ingredients (except spices and salt) and stir well. Add seasonings and salt to taste. With slightly wet hands, pack dough tightly into 6 patties. Fry burgers in a bit of coconut oil in a skillet over medium heat for about 5 minutes on each side. Or, bake for 30 minutes (15 minutes on each side) at 350 degrees until browned. To grill, bake for 5–8 minutes at 350 degrees before placing over coals. Serve on gluten-free buns (see page 131). Makes 6 burgers.

TESLA'S RICE

2 tablespoons sunflower oil

½ cup hazelnut meal

2 tablespoons nutritional yeast

¼ alder smoked sea salt

Fresh ground black pepper

1 leek, thinly sliced

2 carrots, grated

1 stalk celery, thinly sliced

1 1" piece ginger root, peeled and minced

1 cup cooked brown basmati rice

1 cup cooked white basmati rice

1 tablespoon tamari

Tesla was a dog we adopted from the animal shelter in 2010. His difficult story is featured in *Blue Moon Vegetarian*. This rice dish was created in honor of him and originally included eggs, but the hazelnut meal creates such an interesting contrast to the ginger and leek that I like this version much better.

Heat 1 tablespoon of oil in a large skillet over high heat. Add nut meal and nutritional yeast. Season with salt and pepper. When cooked through, transfer to a plate lined with paper towels. Heat remaining tablespoon of oil in skillet over medium heat. Add vegetables and ginger, and then stir-fry until soft. Add rice and tofu; toss with vegetables. Add tamari and toss again. Makes 2 servings.

PHIL'S FABULOUS THREE-BEAN NACHOS

GUACAMOLE

4 ripe Haas avocados

1 tablespoon Vegenaise®

2 tablespoons plain coconut milk yogurt

2 tablespoons lime juice

Garlic granules to taste

Fresh ground black pepper

Tony Chachere's® Original Creole Seasoning to taste

NACHOS

1 ½ cups leftover cooked kidney beans

1 ½ cups leftover cooked pinto beans

1 ½ cups leftover cooked black beans

1 fresh jalapeño

2 tablespoons butter

1 teaspoon cumin

Gluten-free tortilla chips of your choice

Salsa of your choice

1 cup vegan cheddar cheese or Can't Be Cheese (see page 95)

Probably no need to explain this one, except to say: New Year's Day football and Super Bowl parties.

TO MAKE THE GUACAMOLE: Mash avocado with a fork. Blend with yogurt, Vegenaise®, and lime juice until creamy and smooth. Add seasonings to taste. Cover and place in fridge.

TO MAKE THE NACHOS: Preheat oven to 325 degrees. Cook and mash beans in a skillet until well blended. Split jalapeño in half, de-seed at least one half, and then slice all of it into ¼" rings. In a small skillet, melt butter and stir in cumin. Add sliced jalapeño, cook for 5 minutes, and set aside. Spread a layer of chips on a pizza pan, and then top with a third of the grated cheese. Spread a layer of half the beans and then half the jalapeños over the chips and cheese. Add another layer of chips, another third of the cheese, the remaining beans, and the remaining jalapeños, and then top with rest of the cheese. Bake for 10 minutes or until cheese is melted. Top with salsa and guacamole.

IMPOSSIBLE BURGERS

1 cup firm tofu

2 tablespoons nutritional yeast

2 cups gluten-free oats, ground to flour

1 medium-sized red potato, boiled

1 medium-sized onion

1 cup pumpkin seeds, ground

2 teaspoons xanthan gum

2 flax eggs (see page 24)

White rice flour

Fresh ground black pepper to taste

Tony Chachere's® Original Creole Seasoning to taste

Various condiments

Vegan cheese

Lettuce

Tomatoes

In *Blue Moon Vegetarian*, I tell the story of a young woman at our local food co-op who, unbidden, in the middle of the herb aisle, told me about discovering and making cottage cheese burgers. I couldn't resist creating my own version, which I called Oatmeal-Cottage-Cheese Burgers. They had a wonderful flavor, but I considered leaving them out of this book since I already had so many burger recipes. Then I tried them with tofu and nutritional yeast and decided they had to be included, if for no other reason than the fact that they provide a delicious burger alternative for folks who do not or cannot eat nuts, which the other burgers in this book require.

Place all ingredients except flour, salt, and pepper in a food processor and combine. Scoop into a medium-sized bowl. Add flour by hand as necessary to thicken into a moldable consistency. Allow to rest in the refrigerator for 30 minutes. Form into 4–6 patties. Season lightly on each side. Fry or grill. Serve on gluten-free buns (see page 131) with your favorite condiments, cheese, lettuce, and tomatoes.

PHIL'S WEST TEXAS GREEK COMPANY SUPPER

TOFU FETA

8 ounces firm tofu

1 tablespoon lemon juice

1 teaspoon sea salt

2 tablespoons nutritional yeast

PASTA

¼ cup extra-virgin olive oil

12 whole garlic cloves

1 zucchini, cubed

1 yellow winter squash, cubed

1 red bell pepper, cubed

1 red onion, cubed

1 pint whole cherry tomatoes

1 12-ounce package gluten-free pennoni rigate

½ cup pine nuts

Fresh basil leaves, torn into bite-size pieces

The story behind this title goes something like this: Phil lived in Texas for many years. This dish was one a colleague made for potlucks, and it was so yummy and so popular that when the woman moved away, Phil acquired the recipe and made it into one of his specialties. So, I suggested we call it South Texas Company Supper, to which he quickly pointed out that where he had lived, people would not take kindly to that definition. "It's West Texas," he said. "Make no mistake about it." So, okay, but the original recipe also used sheep's milk feta, and sheep's milk feta is Greek. So…

TO MAKE THE TOFU FETA: Process tofu with lemon juice, sea salt, and nutritional yeast in a food processor. Allow to rest overnight before using.

TO MAKE THE PASTA: Preheat oven to 350 degrees. Heat oil in oven in a glass 9" x 13" baking dish until oil is very hot. Remove from oven and stir in garlic. Return to oven and bake until you can smell the garlic, about 15 minutes. Add vegetables to oil and garlic and combine well. Bake another 10 minutes or until vegetables just begin to soften. Do not overbake. Meanwhile, cook ziti according to package directions. Brown pine nuts in dry pan over medium heat until toast colored. Place cooked ziti in a serving dish. Pour vegetables on top of ziti. Top with torn basil leaves, and then sprinkle with toasted pine nuts and tofu feta. Serve immediately. When well covered, keeps in the fridge for up to a week. Makes 8–12 servings.

THREE-BEAN CHEESY SPOONBREAD

BEANS

1 cup dried black beans

1 cup dried pinto beans

1 cup dried kidney beans

6 quarts water

1 tablespoon yellow mustard

1 tablespoon garlic granules

2 teaspoons rosemary, crushed

1 teaspoon cardamom

Crushed chipotle chili peppers to taste

Sea salt to taste

Fresh ground black pepper to taste

SPOONBREAD

2 flax eggs (see page 24)

171 grams cornmeal

95 grams almond flour

111 grams oat flour

57 grams tapioca flour

1 teaspoon baking powder

½ teaspoon salt

¼ cup plus 2 tablespoons sunflower oil

1 teaspoon xanthan gum

1 tablespoon agave syrup

1 cup unsweetened coconut milk beverage

2 tablespoons nutritional yeast

½ cup melted vegan butter

Here's the scenario: winter, snow on the ground, candles on the hearth, the beans simmering all afternoon on top of the woodstove.

TO MAKE THE BEANS: Place beans in a large soup pot. Cover with 3 quarts of the water and bring to a boil. Remove from heat and allow to cool. Drain. Return beans to pot and cover with remaining water. Cook on low heat for 1–2 hours, until just starting to soften, making sure there is plenty of water left to form a juice. Add herbs and seasoning. Simmer on very low heat, covered, for 2–3 hours. Allow to cool while baking spoonbread.

TO MAKE THE SPOONBREAD: Prepare flax eggs and set aside. Stir together flours, cornmeal, baking powder, and sea salt. Make a well and add ¼ cup oil, flax eggs, agave, milk, nutritional yeast, and the melted butter. Stir, adding water until a thick batter forms. Oil cast iron skillet with 2 tablespoons sunflower oil. Pour batter in skillet. Cook covered over very low heat on stovetop until bread is firm, about 45 minutes. Place in oven on low broil until golden brown. Allow bread to set up until completely cool, about two hours or overnight.

TO RE-WARM: Warm beans over medium heat on the stove and spoonbread in the oven at 250 degrees. Use a large serving spoon to lift portions of spoonbread into bowls and ladle beans over bread. Top with ketchup and hot sauce as desired. Makes 8 hearty servings.

EAST MEETS WEST BURRITOS

2 cups leftover cooked pinto beans

2 cups leftover cooked black beans

1 tablespoon garlic granules

1 – 2 jalapeños, finely diced

½ cup chopped onions

1 ½ cups cooked white basmati rice

1 batch Surprising Tortillas (see page 96)

1 head endive, chopped

1 ½ cups bok choy, shredded

Sunflower seeds

Kirkland Signature™ Mild Organic Salsa

Shredded vegan cheddar cheese

A good way to use leftover endive and bok choy from Endive and Bok Choy in Creamy Basil-Grapefruit Vinaigrette (see page 55), or vice versa.

Toast sunflower seeds by placing in the oven on a cookie sheet at 250 degrees. In a large skillet over medium heat, mash, stir, and cook beans, garlic, jalapeños, and onion. Layer beans and rice in flat tortillas and add small portions of remaining ingredients. Sprinkle with a handful of sunflower seeds. Fold over ends and roll into burritos. Makes 6 servings.

PAULA'S LASAGNA AL FORNO

SAUCE

¼ cup extra-virgin olive oil

2 medium-sized red onions, chopped

4 cloves garlic, mashed

1 bell pepper, chopped

3 carrots, grated

3 bay leaves

1 tablespoon oregano

2 teaspoons thyme

1 tablespoon basil

2 teaspoons rosemary

2 teaspoons fennel

½ cup dried parsley

2 tablespoons paprika

6 cups chopped fresh tomatoes

2 6-ounce cans tomato paste

1 teaspoon fresh ground black pepper

2 tablespoons agave syrup

Vegetable broth

LASAGNA

1 pound gluten-free lasagna noodles

2 cups toasted walnuts, chopped

8 ounces firm tofu

½ cup nutritional yeast

1 teaspoon sea salt

2 bunches fresh spinach, chopped

1 pound vegan mozzarella cheese

The day in the early 1980s when I found *Laurel's Kitchen* was the day I understood I was not alone in the world and that there were other people who thought about life as I did. I've made the lasagna from that book a thousand times and have canned hundreds of quarts of the sauce, tweaking here and there over the decades until it barely resembles the original recipe. I never thought about reaching out to those authors, but I've bought many copies of their book to give away, and I've recommended it to hundreds of people. It would be impossible in this small space to explain what the discovery of that book meant to me, but one day I will write the book that does.

TO MAKE THE SAUCE: Sauté onion, garlic, and pepper in olive oil over medium heat until onion just begins to caramelize. Stir in carrots and herbs and cook until pungent, about another 10–15 minutes. Add tomatoes, tomato paste, black pepper, and agave syrup. Thin with broth as needed. Cover and simmer for 20–30 minutes.

TO MAKE THE LASAGNA: Preheat oven to 325 degrees. Mix tofu with nutritional yeast and salt. Spread a layer of sauce on the bottom of a Dutch oven. (Baking dishes are too shallow.) Lay enough dry lasagna noodles on top of sauce to cover it. Spread half of tofu mix on top of the noodles for the next layer. Top with ⅓ of the nuts. Add another layer of sauce, and then another layer of noodles, making sure the noodles run the opposite direction of the first layer. Spread spinach over the noodles and top with sliced mozzarella, saving enough to grate for the top. Add another layer of sauce, and then more noodles, again changing the direction of the noodles. Spread the rest of the tofu mix on the noodles next and another ⅓ of the nuts. Add a final layer of noodles in the alternate direction, and then add more sauce. Top with the rest of the mozzarella, grated, and the rest of the nuts. Cover with foil held in place by the Dutch oven lid. Bake for 1 hour. Let sit covered for 30 minutes before serving. Makes 8–12 servings.

SPICY GOULASH

- 2 tablespoons extra-virgin olive oil
- 2 tablespoons sunflower oil
- ½ red bell pepper, chopped
- 6 cloves garlic, minced
- 1 cup chopped celery
- 1 teaspoon dried basil
- 2 bay leaves
- 1 cup leftover Tesla's Rice (see page 111)
- 3 cups leftover Sweet Lentil Polou (see page 102)
- Filtered water
- ¼ teaspoon Tony Chachere's® Original Creole Seasoning
- Pinch dried red chili seeds
- Sea salt to taste
- Fresh ground black pepper to taste
- 1 cup vegan cheddar cheese
- 1 cup chopped bok choy
- ½ cup chopped leek

As with several recipes in this book, this one makes the best of leftovers.

Combine oils in a large frying pan and sauté bell pepper, garlic, and celery over medium heat until partially soft. Add basil and bay leaves. Add leftover rice and polou and enough water to make a liquid mush. Bring to boil and cover. Simmer for 20–30 minutes or until all liquid is absorbed. Add seasonings to taste. Allow to rest, covered and with heat off, for 10 minutes. Add cheese and stir. Add leek and bok choy just before serving. Makes 4 large servings.

BLOODROOT STEW WITH GRILLED SUNFLOWER SANDWICHES

STEW

3 pounds baby beets, peeled and halved

1 large Walla Walla sweet onion, very coarsely chopped

6 cloves elephant garlic, muddled

2 pounds freshly picked young carrots, sliced

2 pounds baby red potatoes, halved

1 quart filtered water

SANDWICHES

4 slices fresh artisan potato sourdough gluten-free bread

4 tablespoons vegan butter

4 tablespoons vegan Monterey Jack cheese

2 tablespoons sunflower seed butter

Beets and bloodroot are not the same thing, but I named this dish because of its color. And if you have never had a grilled sunflower butter sandwich, well, you have just flat missed out on one of life's most delectable gifts.

TO MAKE THE STEW: Blanch stew ingredients in water for 10 minutes. Cover and simmer until beets are soft. Allow to rest 15 minutes.

TO MAKE THE SANDWICHES: While stew is resting, melt 2 tablespoons butter on griddle. For each sandwich, take two slices of bread and spread 1 ½ tablespoons butter on one side of each slice. Place non-buttered side down onto melted butter on griddle. When the griddle sides are browned, flip the slices. Spread 1 tablespoon sunflower seed butter on the browned side of one slice; spread cheese on the browned side of the other slice. Put cheese side and sunflower butter side of sandwich together. Continue grilling sandwich on both sides, flipping regularly, until both are evenly browned. Makes 4 half-sandwiches and 4 plentiful bowls of stew.

OAT-WALNUT BURGERS

3 flax eggs (see page 24)

2 cups walnut pieces, ground to meal

2 cups gluten-free rolled oats

½ cup canned coconut milk

1 large onion, finely chopped

2 teaspoons xanthan gum

½ teaspoon ground sage

1 teaspoon sea salt

Fresh ground black pepper to taste

Chickpea flour

Sunflower oil

3 cups vegetable stock

I have one friend who, once she found this recipe in *Blue Moon Vegetarian*, began flavoring Oat-Walnut Burger with sage and using it like you might sausage. I liked the taste of it so much, I added a small amount to the basic recipe.

Prepare flax eggs and combine with walnuts, oats, milk, onion, xanthan gum, sage, salt, and pepper. Add chickpea flour as necessary to make a thick, moldable consistency. Set half the mixture aside to refrigerate and save for other dishes, or form the entire batch into hamburger-sized patties. Brown patties on both sides in a lightly oiled skillet, and then pour the stock in around them and bring to a boil. Reduce heat and simmer, covered, for 25 minutes. Serve on gluten-free buns (see page 131) and dress as you would a beef burger, or crumble and use as you would ground beef in chili or spaghetti. Makes 8 burgers.

RED-HOT, FOUR-STAR, TWO-BEAN BURRITOS

BEANS

1 ½ cup leftover cooked pinto beans

1 ½ cup leftover cooked black beans

1 tablespoon sunflower oil

1 tablespoon vegan butter

Sea salt to taste

RICE

1 cup cooked white organic basmati rice

2 tablespoons extra-virgin olive oil

½ large green pepper, finely chopped

½ red onion, finely chopped

6 cloves garlic, minced

½ teaspoon ground cumin

¼ teaspoon ground red chili powder

⅛ teaspoon celery salt

¼ cup plain tomato sauce

2 cups cold filtered or spring water

BURRITOS

1 batch Surprising Tortillas (see page 96)

Vegan Monterey Jack cheese, shredded

Plain coconut milk yogurt

Green chili sauce

1 small jicama, diced

1 avocado, diced

Phil lived for sixteen years in West Texas and learned to love hot, hot foods. Me, not so much, but these burritos have nearly made me a convert. It was the addition of jicama and avocado that got me.

TO MAKE THE BEANS: Heat sunflower oil in a frying pan over medium heat. Add butter and allow to melt. Add beans. Mash beans with fork or potato masher and add salt to taste. Fry until beans are heated thoroughly and dry. Cover and set aside.

TO MAKE THE RICE: Heat olive oil in a frying pan over medium heat. Add green pepper, onion, and garlic. Sauté until onion is clear. Add cooked rice, cumin, ground chilies, and celery salt, stirring constantly until rice starts to brown. Add tomato sauce and stir until heated through. Add water. Heat over medium heat to boiling. Set heat to lowest setting and cover. Check at 20 minutes. Cook until rice flakes apart with a fork.

TO MAKE THE BURRITOS: Set oven to 425 degrees. Preheat pizza stone. Warm tortillas one at a time on stone. Layer with beans, rice, cheese, yogurt, chili sauce, jicama, and avocado. Roll burrito-fashion and have a glass of coconut milk close by when eating.

EVERYDAY GRILLING BURGERS

1 ½ cups leftover beans of any kind

1 cup gluten-free whole oats, ground into flour

½ cup nuts of any kind, ground into meal

1 small onion, coarsely chopped

2 tablespoons potato starch mixed with 2 tablespoons water

1 ½ teaspoon sea salt

2 teaspoons garlic granules

2 teaspoons medium chili powder

¼ teaspoon fresh ground pepper

1 cup gluten-free whole oats, processed briefly

1 tablespoon Sriracha sauce or grilling sauce of choice

½ cup yellow split pea flour

2 tablespoons coconut oil

This is another one of those "what's in the cupboard" recipes that I invented one night when we wanted something easy. I called them grilling burgers because they do double duty: they give us an excuse to set up the grill. Yes, and we do grill in the winter—best time for it. Excellent camping burger to make ahead of time, freeze, and then throw on tinfoil over coals. When you freeze them, be sure to put a square of parchment paper between them to keep them from sticking to each other.

Process first 4 ingredients in food processor into a smooth paste. Add potato starch and water mix. Add seasonings. Transfer to medium-sized mixing bowl. Add oats and yellow split pea flour to form thick but somewhat still moist dough. Add more oats and yellow split pea flour in equal amounts as necessary. Cook over low coals, flipping from time to time until toasty brown and heated through. Makes 6 large or 8 medium-sized burgers.

NOT MEAT LOAF

2 flax eggs (see page 24)

2 tablespoons sunflower oil

1 white onion, minced

1 tablespoon butter

2 cups French green lentils, cooked until very soft

½ cup hulled hemp seed

½ cup gluten-free pretzels, finely ground

¾ cup walnuts

½ teaspoon ground thyme

3 tablespoons brown rice flour

½ cup vegetable broth

¼ cup canned coconut milk

2 teaspoons organic white vinegar

2 teaspoons tamari sauce

2 teaspoons xanthan gum

Ketchup

Toasted sunflower seeds, crushed

This title should be self-explanatory. It's not meat, but you won't believe it's not.

Prepare flax eggs and set aside. Toast walnuts in a 225-degree oven until very dark. Begin checking color after 30 minutes. Preheat oven to 325 degrees. Sauté onion in oil until transparent and partially browned. Stir in butter until melted. In a large mixing bowl, add all ingredients (including onions) except flax eggs and sunflower seeds and mix well. Then stir in flax eggs. Once the mixture is somewhat cool, pour into a buttered loaf pan. Bake, covered with foil, for 30 minutes or until set. Remove foil and sprinkle with sunflower seeds. Continue baking until browned around the edges and separated from the pan. Serve with mashed potatoes and Red-Eye Gravy (see page 44) for a truly decadent main course. Makes 6 servings.

LOTUS TOFU IN SWEET SESAME SAUCE

1 package extra-firm tofu, frozen, thawed, and drained (see page 32)

1 cup yellow split pea flour

1 teaspoon sea salt

½ cup unsweetened coconut milk beverage

½ cup toasted sesame oil

¼ cup sesame oil

¼ cup unsalted vegetable broth

2 tablespoons agave syrup

2 teaspoons rice wine vinegar

1 teaspoon arrowroot powder

1 teaspoon low-sodium tamari

1 cup filtered water

Sriracha sauce to taste

½ – ¾ cup cooked white basmati rice for each serving

I call this "Lotus Tofu" because I'm trying to mimic a dish by the same name that I ate at Panda Gardens in Boise. Lotus flour is impossible to find, even on the Internet, but I found that yellow split pea flour tastes very much the same, albeit absent the higher spiritual implications. Tofu prepared this way is wonderfully crunchy and is the way we prepare it for stir fry, but I do admit to being quite passionate about using it as a reason to make Sweet Sesame Sauce. This is one occasion where I prefer white basmati over brown.

Cut tofu into 1" cubes. Mix flour and salt and sift into small bowl. Dip tofu cubes in coconut milk, and then dredge cubes in flour mixture. In frying pan or wok, blend oils and heat over medium heat. Fry coated tofu until crisp, turning as needed. Drain on paper towels. Remove oil from heat and allow to cool slightly. Whisk together broth and agave syrup with leftover oil. Heat through on very low heat. Stir in arrowroot. Add tamari and water. Stir until thickened. Add water as needed to make a slightly thickened sauce. Add dash Sriracha sauce. Stir. Drizzle mixture over fried tofu. Serve on a bed of white basmati rice. Makes 3–4 servings.

RICE BOWL WITH ASIAN EVERYTHING SAUCE

ASIAN EVERYTHING SAUCE

1 12-ounce canned coconut milk

8 ounces filtered water

¼ teaspoon asafetida powder

¼ teaspoon coriander

¼ teaspoon cumin

¼ teaspoon white pepper

½ teaspoon garlic powder

½ teaspoon ginger powder

½ teaspoon mango powder

1 teaspoon channa masala

1 teaspoon yellow curry powder

1 ½ teaspoons tamari

1 tablespoon lime juice

1 tablespoon agave syrup

1 ½ tablespoons mustard

1 ½ teaspoons arrowroot powder

RICE BOWL

2 cups leftover cooked brown Basmati rice

1 8-ounce package tempeh

2 tablespoons toasted sesame oil

½ teaspoon alder smoked sea salt

Assorted steamed vegetables

Cashews

This is leftovers fit for company, thanks to Asian Everything Sauce, which is perfect to make ahead of time and keep in the fridge—just right for those nights when no one wants to cook.

TO MAKE THE SAUCE: Over low heat, whisk all ingredients except arrowroot together in a medium-sized sauce pan. Whisk in arrowroot ½ teaspoon at a time. Allow to thicken. Store refrigerated for up to 2 weeks.

TO MAKE THE RICE BOWL: Heat oil in a small frying pan and crumble in tempeh and salt. Cook until toasty brown. Assemble rice and steamed vegetables in a bowl. Add tempeh. Top with Asian Everything Sauce and cashews. Makes 3–4 servings.

IN-A-PINCH BEAN BOWL

IN-A-PINCH DRESSING

¼ cup unsweetened coconut milk beverage

¼ cup Vegenaise®

¼ cup tahini

2 tablespoons sesame oil

4 teaspoons mustard

4 teaspoons low-sodium tamari

4 teaspoons agave syrup

¼ teaspoon garlic granules

¼ teaspoon Louisiana Red Hot Sauce

¼ teaspoon fresh cracked black pepper

¼ teaspoon tarragon

SALAD

Mixed greens and lettuce

Leftover beans or Five Beans (see page 109)

Sliced carrot

Sliced celery

Sliced cucumber

Chopped onion or leek

Chopped jicama

Chopped avocado

Chopped tomato

Sunflower seeds

Cashews

Another way to clear out leftovers, this main-course salad makes use of whatever greens, raw veggies, and nuts you have on hand, plus leftover beans or Five Beans. It is our "go-to" after-work dish when no one wants to cook, so much so that we buy salad ingredients and cook beans just so we can make it. We served it at a family cabin weekend several years ago to rave reviews.

TO MAKE THE DRESSING: Process ingredients in a blender or small food processor. Cover and refrigerate. Keeps for up to a week.

TO MAKE EACH SALAD BOWL: Prepare bed of lettuce and greens, torn to bite-sized pieces. Layer carrots, celery, cucumber, jicama, and whatever other raw vegetables you desire. Top with ¾ cup beans, followed by onion, avocado, and tomato. Garnish with sunflower seeds, cashews or other nuts, and In-a-Pinch Dressing.

OATMEAL-WALNUT LOAF

½ recipe Oat-Walnut Burgers (see page 120)

½ cup leftover beans, any kind, mashed

¼ cup hulled hemp seed

¼ cup ketchup

Water

It may seem silly to have two recipes for a meat-loaf style dish in the same cookbook, but this one makes good use of leftovers and doesn't require quite the same prep time as Not Meat Loaf (see page 123). I'd be hard pressed to recommend one over the other based just on taste and texture, however.

Preheat oven to 325 degrees. Mix first three ingredients very well and place in loaf pan. Decorate with ketchup. Place a few tablespoons water around bottom inside edges of pan. Cover with foil. Bake for 40 minutes, and then remove foil and allow to bake another 10 or so minutes, or until edges of loaf are golden. Makes 4 servings.

FROM THE BAKERY

I am so honored to be able to include Jan Calvert's Bridge Baking Company recipes in Blue Moon Vegan. Simply put, the woman knows what she is doing. Some notes: nondairy milk refers to unsweetened soy milk, almond milk, coconut milk, etc. Vegan margarine refers to the stick kind, not from a tub. Sugar refers to organic cane sugar. And, although Jan says she believes it would be just fine to substitute agave for honey and vice versa, she is also quick to say that she has not tested this theory. Additionally, notice that Jan uses non-stick spray instead of a Misto®. They should be interchangeable, but, as with all things, without having tested it out, we cannot make guarantees. I recommend reviewing the section A Note about Gluten-Free Baking (see page 15) before proceeding.

WHITE SANDWICH BREAD

390 grams 50/50 flour blend

1 ¼ teaspoons xanthan gum

1 ¼ teaspoons guar gum

¾ teaspoon sea salt

2 + 1 tablespoons organic cane sugar

2 ½ teaspoons active dry yeast

1 ¼ cups nondairy milk

56 grams canola oil

3 egg equivalents (flax eggs or Ener-G® Egg Replacer™—see page 24)

This recipe from Bridge Baking Company is my favorite of Jan's breads. It keeps very well in the refrigerator and makes excellent toast.

TO PREPARE: Spray an 8 ½ x 4 ½" loaf pan with nonstick spray. Warm 1 ¼ cups nondairy milk to 105–110 degrees. In the mixing bowl of a stand mixer fitted with a paddle (not the bread hook), stir together flour blend, xanthan and guar gums, sea salt and 2 tablespoons sugar. In a small bowl, prepare flax eggs or egg replacer for 3 egg equivalents.

TO PROOF THE YEAST: In a small bowl, combine yeast and 1 tablespoon sugar. Whisk in ¼ cup warmed nondairy milk. Let proof until foamy, 7–10 minutes.

TO MIX: In a small bowl, whisk canola oil with remaining 1 cup warmed nondairy milk. With mixer on low, add the proofed yeast mixture to dry dough ingredients in the mixing bowl. Stir in the egg equivalent mixture, and then slowly add the oil and milk mixture. Stir until well combined. The dough will be the consistency of a heavy muffin batter. Beat at medium speed for 4 minutes.

TO LET RISE: Scoop the dough into the prepared loaf pan. Using wet fingers or a spatula dipped in water, smooth the top of the dough. Cover lightly and let rise in a draft-free location for 30–40 minutes, or until the crown of the dough is just slightly above the top of the pan. While the bread is rising, preheat the oven to 375 degrees.

TO BAKE: Using a razor blade or very sharp knife, make 3 diagonal slashes on the top of the loaf. Bake for 10 minutes, and then cover with foil. Bake for another 30–40 minutes, or until the bread is crusty and browned and the internal temperature is 205 degrees.

Remove pan from oven and place on its side on a cooling rack. Let bread cool in pan for 5 minutes, and then remove loaf from pan and return the loaf to the cooling rack, laying it on the opposite side. Allow to cool completely before slicing, 2–3 hours. Makes one loaf.

HONEY OAT SANDWICH BREAD

355 grams 50/50 flour blend

147 grams oat flour

1 ½ teaspoons xanthan gum

1 ½ teaspoons guar gum

1 teaspoon sea salt

3 tablespoons + 1 teaspoon ground gluten-free oats

2 teaspoons active dry yeast

1 ¾ cups nondairy milk

1 tablespoon honey or organic cane sugar

4 tablespoons vegan margarine

80 grams honey

3 egg equivalents (flax eggs or Ener-G® Egg Replacer™—see page 24)

Honey Oat Sandwich Bread is Bridge Baking Company's best-selling bread and the main one they use for sandwiches in the shop. If you've had troubles baking gluten-free bread, this one will turn things around for you.

TO PREPARE: Spray a 9" x 5" loaf pan with nonstick spray. Warm 1 ¾ cups nondairy milk to 105–110°F. Using a food processor, pulse ¼ cup oats briefly. In the mixing bowl of a stand mixer fitted with a paddle (not the bread hook), stir together flour blend, oat flour, xanthan and guar gums, sea salt and 3 tablespoons of the ground oats. In a small bowl, prepare flax eggs or egg replacer for 3 egg equivalents. Melt vegan margarine, and then pour into a medium-sized bowl and allow to cool slightly. Add honey to melted margarine; stir to combine.

TO PROOF THE YEAST: In a small bowl, combine yeast and 1 tablespoon honey or sugar. Whisk in ¼ cup of the warmed nondairy milk. Let proof until foamy, 7–10 minutes.

TO MIX: Add 1 cup of the warmed nondairy milk (reserving ½ cup) to the margarine and honey; stir to combine. With mixer on low, add the proofed yeast mixture to the dry dough ingredients in the mixing bowl. Stir in the egg equivalent mixture, and then slowly add the margarine, honey, and milk mixture. Stir until well combined. The dough will be the consistency of a heavy muffin batter. If needed, add the remaining ½ cup warmed milk, 1 tablespoon at a time, until the dough is the desired consistency. Once all ingredients are well combined, beat at medium-high speed for 8 minutes.

TO LET RISE: Scoop the dough into the prepared loaf pan. Using wet fingers or a spatula dipped in water, smooth the top of the dough. Sprinkle some of the remaining ground oats on the top of the loaf. Cover lightly and let rise in a draft-free location for 30–40 minutes, or until the crown of the dough is just slightly above the top of the pan. While the bread is rising, preheat the oven to 350 degrees.

TO BAKE: Using a razor blade or very sharp knife, make 3 diagonal slashes on the top of the loaf. Bake for 10 minutes, and then cover with foil. Bake for another 30–40 minutes, or until the bread is crusty and browned and the internal temperature is 207 degrees. Remove pan from oven and place on its side on a cooling rack. Let bread cool in pan for 5 minutes, and then remove loaf from pan and return the loaf to the cooling rack, laying it on the opposite side. Allow to cool completely before slicing, 2–3 hours. Makes one loaf.

BURGER BUNS

156 grams 70/30 flour blend

54 grams sweet rice flour

1 ½ teaspoons xanthan gum

2 teaspoons baking powder

½ teaspoons sea salt

1 tablespoons active dry yeast

2 tablespoons organic cane sugar

1 cup filtered water

1 egg equivalents (flax eggs or Ener-G® Egg Replacer™—see page 24)

56 grams canola oil

½ teaspoon apple cider vinegar

What? A cookbook with four burger recipes and you thought we'd send you to the store for buns? Jan Calvert has us covered. These buns are a treat unto themselves.

TO PREPARE: Spray 6 sections of a hamburger bun pan with nonstick spray. Alternatively, spray 6 English muffin rings with nonstick spray and place on a parchment-lined baking sheet. Warm 1 cup water to 105–110 degrees. In a medium-sized bowl, whisk together all dry ingredients. In the mixing bowl of a stand mixer fitted with a paddle (not the bread hook), prepare the egg equivalent, and then stir in canola oil and vinegar.

TO PROOF THE YEAST: In a medium bowl, combine yeast and sugar. Whisk in the warmed water. Let proof until foamy, 7–10 minutes.

TO MIX: Slowly add proofed yeast to the mixing bowl; mix briefly. Add flour mixture gradually, mixing after each addition. The dough will be soft and sticky. Beat at medium-high speed for 3 minutes.

TO LET RISE: Divide the dough evenly into the prepared pan or rings, smoothing tops of dough with wet fingers. Cover lightly and let rise in a draft-free location for 30–45 minutes, or until doubled in size. While the buns are rising, preheat the oven to 375 degrees.

TO BAKE: Bake for 10 minutes, and then rotate pan 180 degrees. Bake another 8–10 minutes, or until golden brown. Do not under-bake.

Remove pan from oven and place on a cooling rack. Cool buns in pan for 5 minutes, and then remove from pan or rings and return buns to the cooling rack. Allow to cool completely before slicing. Makes 6 buns.

FOCACCIA

BREAD

174 grams 35/65 flour blend

10 grams masa harina

1 teaspoon xanthan gum

1 teaspoon guar gum

1 teaspoon dried rosemary, chopped

1 teaspoon Italian herb seasoning

¾ teaspoon sea salt

1 ½ teaspoons active dry yeast

¼ cup + ½ cup filtered water

1 teaspoon honey or organic cane sugar

30 grams extra-virgin olive oil

2 egg equivalents (flax eggs or Ener-G® Egg Replacer™—see page 24)

½ teaspoon vinegar

When Jan told me she was including a focaccia recipe, I was incredulous. Yet one more thing I assumed I'd never eat again. Great for veggie sandwiches, but when it comes to focaccia, I'm more inclined to eat it plain.

TO PREPARE: Spray an 8" x 8" pan with nonstick spray. Warm ¾ cup water to 105–110 degrees. In the mixing bowl of a stand mixer fitted with a paddle (not the bread hook), stir together flour blend, masa harina, xanthan and guar gums, rosemary, Italian seasoning, and sea salt. In a medium-sized bowl, prepare egg replacer for 2 egg equivalents. In a small bowl, combine all the topping ingredients except the olive oil.

TO PROOF THE YEAST: In a small bowl, combine yeast and 1 teaspoon honey or sugar. Whisk in ¼ cup of the warmed water. Let proof until foamy, 7–10 minutes.

TO MIX: Add olive oil, remaining ½ cup warm water and vinegar to egg replacement mixture; stir to combine. With mixer on low, add the proofed yeast mixture to the dry dough ingredients. Slowly pour in the rest of the liquid ingredients. Stir until well combined. The dough will be soft and sticky. Beat at medium-high speed for 2 minutes.

TO LET RISE: Scoop the dough into the prepared pan. Using wet hands, spread the dough evenly. Drizzle 1 tablespoon olive oil over the top of

TOPPING

1 tablespoon extra-virgin olive oil

½ teaspoon dried rosemary

½ teaspoon dried sage

½ teaspoon dried thyme

½ teaspoon coarse sea salt

¼ teaspoon fresh coarsely ground black pepper

the dough and spread evenly. Using the tips of your fingers, "dimple" the top of the dough. Sprinkle with herb mixture. Cover lightly and let rise in a draft-free location for 40–60 minutes, or until doubled in size. While the focaccia is rising, preheat the oven to 400 degrees.

TO BAKE: Bake for 20-25 minutes, or until golden brown. Remove pan from oven and place on a cooling rack. Let cool in pan for 5 minutes, then remove from pan and return bread to the cooling rack. Makes one loaf.

TO REHEAT: The focaccia is best the day it's made. To reheat, place in a microwave for 10–15 seconds or on a baking sheet in a 300-degree oven for 10–15 minutes. Store tightly wrapped in the refrigerator.

Variation: Sun-dried Tomato Focaccia
Drain oil from ⅓ cup of oil-packed sun-dried tomatoes. Coarsely chop if necessary. Gently fold drained tomatoes into dough just before scooping into pan. For topping, replace rosemary, sage, and thyme with dried basil.

Variation: Caramelized Onion Focaccia
Sprinkle top of focaccia with herb(s) of choice. Then top with 2 cups of chopped, sautéed onions that have been tossed with 1 tablespoon extra-virgin olive oil. Bake as directed.

Variation: Roasted Garlic Focaccia
Before starting focaccia, roast 2 full heads of garlic by separating each head into individual cloves (unpeeled). Toss garlic cloves in 2 tablespoons extra-virgin olive oil, and then place them in a small ovenproof bowl and cover it tightly in foil. Roast in oven at 350 degrees for 30 minutes, or until cloves are soft. Let cool. Squeeze each clove from its peel. Scatter roasted garlic cloves evenly over the top of the prepared focaccia, and then sprinkle it with salt and pepper (omit the other herbs). Allow to rise; bake as directed.

CRUSTY BOULE

396 grams 50/50 flour blend

60 grams oat flour

1 teaspoon xanthan gum

1 teaspoon guar gum

1 teaspoon psyllium husk

1 ½ teaspoons sea salt

1 tablespoon active dry yeast

1 tablespoon organic cane sugar or honey

⅓ cup + 1 cup filtered water

2 egg equivalents (flax eggs or Ener-G® Egg Replacer™—see page 24)

37 grams canola oil

Extra-virgin olive oil

Coarse sea salt

This bread from Bridge Baking Company is the perfect accompaniment to many of the soup recipes in this book. So decadent and astonishing, yet nutritious, vegan, and gluten-free.

TO PREPARE: Warm 1 ⅓ cups water to 105–110 degrees. In the bowl of a stand mixer fitted with a paddle (not the bread hook), stir dry ingredients well. In a small bowl, prepare 2 egg equivalents. In another bowl, combine 1 cup warm water and canola oil.

TO PROOF THE YEAST: In a medium-sized bowl, combine yeast and sugar or honey. Whisk in ⅓ cup of the warmed water. Let proof until foamy, 7–10 minutes.

TO MIX: Slowly add proofed yeast to the dry dough ingredients in the mixing bowl; mix briefly. Add egg equivalent mixture gradually, and then slowly add remaining liquid ingredients. Mix until all ingredients come together.

TO LET RISE: Place dough in a large, clean bowl and cover with a towel or plastic wrap coated with nonstick spray. Let rise for up to 2 hours. After rising, the dough can be formed into two loaves or placed in a large container with a lid and refrigerated. It will keep for up to a week (and refrigerating the dough at least overnight improves the flavor).

TO BAKE: Shape half of the dough (1 pound) into a ball and place on parchment paper. Let rest in a draft-free area for about 45 minutes if dough is room temperature; 1 ½–2 hours if refrigerated. Thirty minutes before rising time is done, place a pizza stone on the middle shelf of the oven and preheat to 450 degrees. If you don't have a pizza stone, place a clay baking dish into oven to preheat.

With a razor blade or serrated knife, make 3 slashes on the top of the loaf, ¼" deep. Drizzle the top with a little olive oil and sprinkle with coarse salt. Keep the dough on the parchment paper and place on pizza stone or into preheated clay baker.

Fill a large sauté pan or cast iron skillet with ice cubes. Put pan on bottom shelf of oven. Bake loaf in oven until the top is lightly browned and the bread feels firm, about 35 minutes, or to 180 degrees. Let bread cool in pan at least 15 minutes before slicing.

Variation: Raisin Fennel Boule

After dividing the dough but before forming it into ball, mix in 2 tablespoons fennel seed and ¾ cup golden raisins. Form dough into ball and continue as above.

Variation: Rosemary Walnut Boule

Finely chop 2 sprigs of rosemary, stems removed. After dividing dough but before forming into ball, mix in chopped rosemary and ¾ cup coarsely chopped walnuts. Form dough into ball and continue as above.

PIZZA CRUST

454 grams 70/30 flour blend

70 grams almond meal

4 ½ teaspoons psyllium husk powder

2 ½ teaspoons baking powder

1 teaspoon Italian herb seasoning

2 teaspoons sea salt

1 teaspoon instant yeast

2 ½ cups filtered water

56 grams vegetable or canola oil

I had assumed I'd never eat pizza again, but now I know that is not the case. Jan Calvert's recipe makes it look easy, but what surprises me most is that you can partially bake the crusts and freeze them. I'd simply never thought of doing that, nor had I ever thought of working Italian herbs into the dough.

TO PREPARE: Line 2 baking sheets with parchment paper. Warm 2 ½ cups water to 105 degrees. In the mixing bowl of a stand mixer fitted with a paddle (not the bread hook), stir together all the dry ingredients, including the instant yeast.

TO MIX: Combine warm water and oil in a medium-sized bowl. With mixer running on low speed, slowly add water and oil in a steady stream to dry dough ingredients until completely combined. Increase speed to medium and beat for 6 minutes. Dough will be sticky and look like thick pancake batter.

TO LET RISE: Scrape dough into a glass bowl and cover with plastic wrap. Place in a draft-free area until inside of dough is bubbly, about 90 minutes. After 1 hour, adjust oven racks to lower and middle positions and preheat oven to 350 degrees.

TO BAKE: Spray parchment-lined baking sheets with nonstick spray. Scrape half of the dough onto the middle of one of the sheets. Oil your hands and spread dough outward from the center into an 11" circle about ¼" thick, leaving the outer edge slightly thicker than the middle. Re-oil your hands as needed. Repeat with the other half of the dough on the other baking sheet.

Place both baking sheets in oven and bake for 10 minutes. Rotate sheets from top to bottom racks of the oven and exchange from right to left, and then continue baking for an additional 10–15 minutes or until the crust is brown on the bottom and just beginning to brown on the top. Transfer crusts to wire racks to cool. Makes 2 crusts.

TO REHEAT: Use crusts within 4 hours, or prepare completely cooled crusts for freezing by wrapping first in plastic wrap, then in foil. Frozen crusts can be topped with desired ingredients and baked in a 500-degree oven without first thawing. Frozen crusts are best used within a month.

MORNING GLORY MUFFINS

280 grams 70/30 flour blend

½ teaspoon xanthan gum

½ teaspoon guar gum

198 grams organic cane sugar

2 teaspoons baking soda

2 teaspoons cinnamon

¼ teaspoons salt

2 cups shredded carrots (from 2–3 carrots)

½ cup raisins

½ cup chopped walnuts

½ cup unsweetened shredded coconut

1 apple, peeled, cored and shredded

2 egg equivalents (flax eggs or Ener-G® Egg Replacer™—see page 24)

½ cup canola or vegetable oil

½ cup unsweetened applesauce

2 teaspoons high-quality vanilla extract

Bridge Baking Company is housed in an old-fashioned diner and sits right across the street from Lewis-Clark State College. If I were a college student, I'd be in there every single morning for a cup of Jan's soul-mending coffee and one of these little nutritional powerhouses. They seriously will get you through the morning, and the flavor and texture is to die for.

TO PREPARE: Preheat oven to 350 degrees. Line muffin tins with paper liners. Sift all dry ingredients into the bowl of a stand mixer fitted with a paddle (not the bread hook); whisk to combine well. In a small bowl, prepare two egg equivalents. In a small bowl, combine oil, applesauce and vanilla.

TO MIX: Fold carrots, raisins, walnuts, coconut, and apple into dry dough ingredients. With mixer on low speed, add egg replacement mixture, and then add other liquid ingredients. Stir until combined, and then increase speed to medium and beat for 2 minutes.

TO BAKE: Scoop batter into prepared tins, filling ⅔ full. Bake for 20 minutes or until a toothpick inserted into center comes out clean, turning pans halfway through baking. Cool muffins in pans on wire rack for 5 minutes, and then remove muffins to a wire rack to finish cooling. Makes 14–16 muffins.

ORANGE ZUCCHINI MUFFINS

MUFFINS

350 grams 70/30 flour blend

35 grams tapioca starch

35 grams sweet rice flour

½ teaspoon xanthan gum

½ teaspoon guar gum

1 teaspoon sea salt (scant)

2 teaspoons baking powder

½ teaspoon baking soda

198 grams organic cane sugar

126 grams unsweetened applesauce

75 grams canola oil

½ teaspoon high-quality vanilla extract

Nondairy milk as needed—approximately 1 cup

1 orange

2 cups zucchini, grated

⅓ cup walnuts or raisins (optional)

GLAZE

½ cup organic powdered sugar

2 teaspoons juice from orange

¼ teaspoon zest from orange

Admit it—you've been looking for a perfect muffin all your life, haven't you? Look no more. Jan's are the holy grail of muffins, guaranteed. My son still refuses to believe these are vegan and gluten-free.

TO PREPARE: Preheat oven to 350 degrees. Line muffin tins with paper liners. In the bowl of a stand mixer fitted with a paddle (not the bread hook), whisk all dry ingredients together. Wash and zest orange; reserve ¼ teaspoon for glaze. Juice the orange; reserve 2 teaspoons for glaze. In a separate bowl, whisk applesauce, canola oil, vanilla, orange juice, and orange zest with ¼ cup of nondairy milk.

TO MIX: With mixer running on low speed, slowly pour liquid ingredients into dry dough ingredients, stirring just until combined. Add additional nondairy milk as needed to create a thick muffin batter. Fold in grated zucchini and nuts or raisins.

TO BAKE: Scoop batter into prepared tins, filling ⅔ full. Bake for 20–25 minutes or until golden and a toothpick inserted into the center comes out clean. Cool muffins in pans on a wire rack for 5 minutes, then remove muffins to wire rack to finish cooling. Makes 14–15 muffins.

TO GLAZE: Whisk together remaining orange juice, powdered sugar and orange zest until combined. Cool muffins for 10 minutes, and then spoon glaze over top.

Variation: Pumpkin Spice Muffins
Add to dry ingredients 1 teaspoon cinnamon, ½ teaspoon ginger, and ¼ teaspoon nutmeg. Replace zucchini with a 15-ounce can of pureed pumpkin. Fold in ¼ cup finely diced crystallized ginger before spooning into muffin liners.

Variation: Carrot Pineapple Coconut Muffins
Strain crushed pineapple from an 8-ounce can, reserving the juice. Use juice to replace orange juice. Replace grated zucchini with grated carrot. Fold drained pineapple, grated carrot, and 1 cup shredded coconut into batter before spooning into muffin liners.

CARROT CAKE

CAKE

245 grams 70/30 flour blend

25 grams sweet rice flour

10 grams brown rice flour

½ teaspoon xanthan gum

½ teaspoon guar gum

2 teaspoons baking powder

2 teaspoons baking soda

½ teaspoon sea salt

2 teaspoons cinnamon

½ teaspoon nutmeg

2 tablespoons Ener-G® Egg Replacer™

½ cup filtered water

168 grams vegetable or canola oil

148 grams organic cane sugar

141 grams organic brown sugar

114 grams orange marmalade

120 grams orange juice

6 medium-sized or 5 large carrots

¾ cup chopped walnuts, toasted

BUTTERCREAM FROSTING

½ cup vegan margarine

½ cup vegan shortening

4 cups organic powdered sugar

1 – 2 tablespoons nondairy milk

½ – 1 tablespoon agave syrup

¾ teaspoon vanilla

I'm pretty certain I have made in the neighborhood of two dozen different carrot cake recipes over the years. Then I tried Jan's and realized I'd never even come close to making a good one. This one deserves a star on the Hollywood Walk of Fame. It's the marmalade and orange juice that skyrockets it into the stratosphere.

TO PREPARE: Preheat oven to 350 degrees. Spray two 8" cake pans with nonstick spray; line the bottom of each pan with parchment paper and spray the parchment. For cupcakes, line muffin tins with paper cupcake liners. Peel and grate carrots; set aside. In a small bowl, whisk Ener-G® Egg Replacer™ with water until frothy. Sift dry ingredients into a medium-sized bowl. Fold in grated carrots and nuts, coating carrots completely.

TO MIX: Combine egg replacer, oil, sugars, marmalade, and orange juice in the bowl of a stand mixer; mix on low until well blended. Stir in dry ingredients 1 cup at a time, blending well after each addition. When fully incorporated, turn mixer to medium and beat for 2 minutes.

TO BAKE: Transfer the batter to prepared pans. Bake for 35–40 minutes for cake or 20–25 minutes for cupcakes, or until a toothpick inserted into the center comes out clean and the top springs back when lightly touched. Do not under-bake, because the cakes or cupcakes will collapse when cooled. Cool cake or cupcakes in pans on a wire rack for 10 minutes, and then remove to wire rack to finish cooling. Makes one 8" 2-layer cake or 12–14 cupcakes.

TO FROST: Allow margarine and shortening to soften to room temperature. Using a hand mixer and starting with lesser amounts of milk and agave syrup, beat all frosting ingredients until smooth, adding remaining amounts of liquids as necessary to reach desired consistency. Spread over cooled cake layers or cupcakes. Makes enough to frost 1 8" 2-layer cake or 12-14 cupcakes.

CHOCOLATE CAKE

CAKE

197 grams 35/65 flour blend

212 grams organic brown sugar

99 grams organic cane sugar

53 grams unsweetened cocoa powder

½ teaspoon xanthan gum

½ teaspoon guar gum

1 tablespoon baking powder

¾ teaspoon sea salt

76 grams vegan margarine

56 grams vegetable or canola oil

1 teaspoon high-quality vanilla extract

1 ½ teaspoon Ener-G® Egg Replacer™

2 tablespoons filtered water

1 cup warm coffee

1 teaspoon apple cider vinegar

CHOCOLATE FROSTING

½ cup vegan margarine

½ cup vegan shortening

3 ½ – 4 cups organic powdered sugar

¾ cup cocoa

1 – 2 tablespoons strong coffee

½ – 1 tablespoons agave syrup

½ teaspoon vanilla

¼ teaspoon almond extract

Proof positive you can have your cake and eat it, too. I never dreamed of spiking chocolate cake with coffee, but the rich undertone makes this dense, moist cake flat dreamy. For my birthday this year, I intend to make it in four half-depth layers with raspberry jam in between.

TO PREPARE: Preheat oven to 350 degrees. Spray two 8" cake pans with nonstick spray; line the bottom of each pan with parchment paper and spray parchment. For cupcakes, line muffin tins with paper cupcake liners. Melt vegan margarine; allow to cool slightly. Add oil and vanilla; stir to combine. In a small bowl, whisk Ener-G® Egg Replacer™ with water until frothy.

TO MIX: Measure dry ingredients into the bowl of a stand mixer fitted with a paddle (not the bread hook). Stir on low speed until well combined. Slowly pour in the melted margarine and oil mixture, then the egg replacer. Stir until the mixture looks crumbly and sandy. Add the apple cider vinegar to the warm coffee; slowly add this mixture in a steady stream to the dough. Once all the liquid is fully incorporated, turn the mixer to medium and beat for 2 minutes. Batter will be thick and smooth.

TO BAKE: Transfer the batter to prepared pans. Bake for 30–35 minutes for cake or 20–25 minutes for cupcakes, or until a toothpick inserted into the center comes out clean and the top springs back when lightly touched. Do not under-bake, because the cakes or cupcakes will collapse when cooled. Cool in pans on a wire rack for 10 minutes, and then remove from pans. Return to wire rack to finish cooling. Makes one 8" 2-layer cake or 12–14 cupcakes.

TO FROST: Allow margarine and shortening to soften to room temperature. Using a hand mixer and starting with lesser amounts of powdered sugar, coffee, and agave syrup, beat all frosting ingredients until smooth, adding remaining amounts of sugar and liquids as necessary to reach desired consistency. Spread over cooled cake layers or cupcakes. Makes enough to frost 1 8" 2-layer cake or 12-14 cupcakes.

CINNAMON ROLLS

FILLING

220 grams organic brown sugar

4 tablespoons vegan margarine, very soft

1 ½ teaspoons xanthan gum

3 tablespoons cinnamon

DOUGH

124 grams sorghum flour

130 grams brown rice flour

72 grams almond meal

85 grams millet flour

100 grams potato starch

100 grams tapioca starch

49 grams sweet rice flour

1 teaspoon xanthan gum

1 teaspoon guar gum

1 teaspoon sea salt

2 ½ teaspoons active dry yeast

1 teaspoon + 2 tablespoons organic cane sugar

½ cup + 1 cup unsweetened non-dairy milk

2 egg equivalents (flax eggs or Ener-G® Egg Replacer™—see page 24)

⅔ cup vegan margarine, melted

1 teaspoon high-quality vanilla extract

1 teaspoon apple cider vinegar

There is not a single big city diner or small-town café in the West that does not boast about its cinnamon rolls, yet I've never cared for them much because they always seem a little dry and dependent on a pool of frosting to cover it up. And, of course, I always felt terrible after eating one. As I mentioned earlier, Jan had me try these out one morning when we were first working on the book, and they so took me aback, I almost cried.

TO PREPARE: In a large bowl, combine all filling ingredients except margarine. Using pastry cutter, 2 knives or your fingers, incorporate softened margarine until well combined. Warm 1 ½ cup nondairy milk to 105–110 degrees. In the mixing bowl of a stand mixer fitted with a paddle (not the bread hook), stir dry ingredients well. In a small bowl, prepare 2 egg equivalents. Melt ⅔ cup vegan margarine; allow to cool slightly. Spray a 9" x 13" baking pan with nonstick spray.

TO PROOF THE YEAST: In a medium-sized bowl, combine yeast and 1 teaspoon sugar. Whisk in ½ cup of the warmed nondairy milk. Let proof until foamy, 7–10 minutes.

TO MIX: In a medium-sized bowl, stir together melted margarine, remaining 1 cup of warmed milk, vanilla, and cider vinegar; set aside. Slowly add proofed yeast to the mixing bowl; mix briefly. Add egg mixture gradually, and then slowly add remaining liquid ingredients. Mix until all ingredients come together. Dough will be thick and sticky. Beat on medium speed for 3 minutes.

TO FORM THE ROLLS: Lay 2 pieces of plastic wrap on a countertop, each about 20" long and overlapping lengthwise by about 2". Sprinkle evenly with 2 tablespoons sugar. Scrape dough onto plastic wrap. Using wet or oiled hands, roughly shape dough into a rectangle. Cover dough with 2 more pieces of overlapped plastic wrap. Using rolling pin, roll dough into a 12" wide rectangle, ½" thick (about 16–18" in length).

GLAZE

2 tablespoons vegan margarine, softened

1 cup organic powdered sugar

½ teaspoon high-quality vanilla extract

2 tablespoons nondairy milk

Carefully remove top layer of plastic wrap. Spread filling mixture evenly over dough and closely to edges, leaving a 1 ½" margin along one short end. Using the bottom layer of plastic wrap, roll dough slowly, starting at the opposite end of the margin, stopping as needed to gently press dough to maintain an even thickness and width. Continue rolling, stopping at the margin. With wet fingers, moisten dough along the margin, and then seal this margin to the roll by pinching and smoothing with wet fingers. Using dental floss, cut the rolled up dough into 1 ½" rolls by carefully sliding floss under the end of the roll, bringing the ends together up and around each side and criss-crossing, as if you were going to tie them, cutting through the dough with the floss. Place rolls in a pan, with sides barely touching, making 2 rows of 4 rolls. Cover loosely with a dish towel or plastic wrap sprayed with nonstick spray.

TO LET RISE: Place pan in a draft-free area and allow to rise until doubled, about 30 minutes. Preheat oven to 350 degrees.

TO BAKE: Bake for 15 minutes. Rotate pan 180 degrees and continue baking until rolls are nicely browned, about another 10–15 minutes. Let rolls cool in pan for 5 minutes, and then transfer them to a serving plate. Makes 8 cinnamon rolls.

TO GLAZE: While rolls are baking, cream margarine in a medium-sized bowl with a handheld mixer (or a strong arm and wooden spoon). Gradually add powdered sugar to incorporate, then vanilla. Thin to desired consistency with nondairy milk. Spread a dollop of glaze on each cinnamon roll while they're still warm.

"GRAHAM" CRACKERS

150 grams 50/50 flour blend

50 grams sweet rice flour

90 grams organic dark brown sugar

½ teaspoon baking soda

½ teaspoon salt

1 teaspoon cinnamon

½ teaspoon xanthan gum

¼ teaspoon guar gum

7 tablespoon vegan margarine, chilled

18 grams filtered ice water, plus more if needed

50 grams honey

15 grams molasses

1 teaspoon high-quality vanilla extract

Graham crackers are another item on the list of things I thought I'd left behind. Jan's are better than any I've ever tasted, and they made me realize what a poor-quality product those store-bought ones actually are.

TO PREPARE: Combine all dry ingredients in the bowl of a food processor and pulse to combine. Cut vegan margarine into ½" cubes and place in the freezer until ready to use. In a small bowl, whisk together ice water, honey, molasses, and vanilla.

TO MIX: Sprinkle cubes of chilled margarine over the top of the dry ingredients in the food processor bowl. Pulse until margarine is combined and mixture is the texture of cornmeal. With processor running, slowly pour liquid mixture through the tube of the food processor, stopping when the dough gathers into a ball. Be careful to not add too much liquid. Scrape dough onto a sheet of plastic wrap; flatten it into a disk and refrigerate for at least 4 hours. Remove dough disk from refrigerator and let stand at room temperature 15–20 minutes, or until soft enough to roll out.

TO CUT SQUARE CRACKERS: Line countertop with parchment or wax paper. Place dough disk on top, and then top dough with another piece of paper. Roll out dough to ⅛" thickness, and then remove top piece of paper. Using a pastry wheel or pizza cutter, cut into 2 ½ x 2 ½" squares. Prick each cracker with a toothpick or the tines of a fork (unless you happen to have a docker—if you do, dock each cracker). Carefully transfer each cracker onto a parchment-lined baking sheet, leaving ½" space between each cracker. Re-roll scraps and repeat.

TO CUT ROUND CRACKERS (BECAUSE IT'S A LOT EASIER): Line a baking sheet with parchment paper. Using a teaspoon or melon ball scoop, form balls of dough that weigh 16 grams each. Place balls onto baking sheet, spaced 3" apart. Cut several 3" squares of wax paper. Using a measuring cup or a flat-bottomed glass, top a ball of dough with the square of wax paper and press until dough is ⅛" thick (basically, until it's the same diameter as the cup or glass you're pressing into it). Repeat for each ball of dough, replacing the wax paper square when it starts to stick to the dough. Prick each cracker with a toothpick or tines of a fork (or roll with docker).

TO BAKE: Refrigerate the pan(s) for at least 15 minutes. Meanwhile, preheat oven to 325 degrees. Bake crackers for 10 minutes, and then rotate pan(s) and continue baking for another 10 minutes or until crisp and set. Cool pan briefly on a wire rack, and then transfer crackers onto wire rack to finish cooling. Store crackers in an airtight container at room temperature for up to 2 weeks. Makes 2 dozen crackers.

COCONUT MACAROONS

COOKIES

120 grams 70/30 flour blend

2 cups unsweetened coconut

3 cups sweetened flaked coconut

½ teaspoon salt

⅔ cups agave syrup

1 cup light canned coconut milk

2 teaspoon high-quality vanilla extract

CHOCOLATE GLAZE

8 ounces vegan, gluten-free dark chocolate chips

1 tablespoon corn syrup (look for organic)

Pinch of sea salt

When Jan told me she'd come up with a vegan macaroon, I couldn't believe it—macaroons are traditionally full of egg whites. And you won't believe it either. This is another recipe I'd suggest making when no one is home, because there's an issue that comes up: you may... you know... feel the uncontrollable urge to overindulge.

TO PREPARE: Preheat oven to 350 degrees.

TO MIX: Combine all cookie ingredients in a large bowl and mix thoroughly with a large spatula. Stir and fold repeatedly, until very well mixed. The dough will be moist and sticky.

TO BAKE: Line a baking sheet with parchment paper or a silicone mat. Dip a cookie scoop or ice cream scoop in water, and then fill the scoop with dough. Make sure the dough is tightly packed so the macaroon will hold together and that the dough is even with the rim so the cookie has a nice flat bottom. Place scooped dough on the prepared baking sheet, using your wet fingers to reshape the macaroon if needed. Repeat with remaining dough. Bake until just turning brown, 10–15 minutes depending on the size of macaroon you've made, and rotating the pan halfway through baking. Let macaroons cool on the baking sheet for 5 minutes, and then transfer them to a wire rack to finish cooling. Makes 20 cookies.

TO GLAZE: After macaroons have cooled completely, line a baking sheet with wax paper. In a small bowl, melt chocolate chips, corn syrup, and a pinch of salt in the microwave in 30-second increments, stirring after each 30 seconds, until the mixture is smooth. Carefully dip the top of each macaroon in the chocolate glaze, using a table knife to scrape off any excess chocolate. Set glazed macaroon on the wax paper to catch any chocolate drips. Let cool until set, 30–45 minutes.

PEANUT BUTTER COOKIES

350 grams 40/60 flour blend

35 grams oat flour

1 teaspoon xanthan gum

½ teaspoon guar gum

½ teaspoon baking soda

½ teaspoon baking powder

1 teaspoon sea salt

1 cup vegan margarine, slightly softened

198 grams organic dark brown sugar

198 grams organic cane sugar

240 grams extra crunchy peanut butter

2 teaspoons high-quality vanilla extract

1 tablespoon Ener-G® Egg Replacer™

¼ cup filtered water

1 ½ cups roasted and salted peanuts, coarsely chopped, divided

I've not very often in my life been called a liar, but that's exactly what happened when a family member tried Jan's Peanut Butter Cookies and I told him they were vegan and gluten-free. These will make you wonder why we all don't bake this way.

TO PREPARE: Sift all dry ingredients into a large bowl; whisk to combine well. In a small bowl, whisk egg replacer and water until frothy. Measure peanut butter into a separate small bowl.

TO MIX: In the bowl of a stand mixer fitted with a paddle (not a bread hook), cream vegan margarine until smooth. Add dark brown sugar and granulated sugar to the margarine, along with ½ cup of the dry ingredient blend; stir to incorporate, and then beat until fluffy (about 3 minutes). Add peanut butter, then egg mixture, then vanilla, and stir to combine. Add the remainder of the dry ingredient blend, ½ cup at a time, until the dough is well blended. Stir in 1 cup of the chopped peanuts. Cover the dough with plastic wrap and refrigerate for at least 24 hours.

TO BAKE: Allow dough to sit at room temperature for 20 minutes or until soft enough to form into balls. Preheat oven to 350 degrees. Form dough into 1 ½" balls, each weighing approximately 36 grams. Roll the tops of the balls in the remaining ½ cup chopped peanuts. Place balls on parchment-lined baking sheets 3" apart. Flatten slightly, making a criss-cross pattern on the top with a fork. Bake until slightly browned on edges and just slightly underdone in the middle, 10–12 minutes, rotating the pan halfway through baking. Leave the cookies on the baking sheet to cool for 5 minutes to set, and then transfer cookies to a wire rack to finish cooling. Store cookies in an airtight container for up to 2 weeks. Makes 4 dozen cookies.

CHOCOLATE CHIP COOKIES

124 grams sorghum flour

114 grams tapioca starch

147 grams potato starch

61 grams oat flour

48 grams almond meal

1 teaspoon xanthan gum

1 teaspoon guar gum

1 ½ teaspoons baking soda

2 teaspoons baking powder

1 teaspoon salt

1 ¼ cups vegan margarine, slightly softened

248 grams organic brown sugar

198 grams granulated cane sugar

2 teaspoons high-quality vanilla extract

1 tablespoon Ener-G® Egg Replacer™

¼ cup filtered water

16 ounces vegan, gluten-free chocolate chips

The same family member who couldn't believe the Peanut Butter Cookies (see page 145) were gluten-free and vegan said the same thing about these.

TO PREPARE: Sift all dry ingredients into a large bowl; whisk to combine well. In a small bowl, whisk egg replacer and water until frothy.

TO MIX: In the bowl of a stand mixer fitted with a paddle (not the bread hook), cream vegan margarine until smooth. Add brown sugar and granulated sugar to the margarine, along with 2 cups of the dry ingredient blend; stir to incorporate, and then beat until fluffy (about 3 minutes). Add egg replacer, then vanilla, and stir to combine. Add the remainder of the dry ingredient blend, ½ cup at a time, until the dough is well blended. Stir in chocolate chips. Cover dough with plastic wrap and refrigerate for at least 36 hours.

TO BAKE: Allow dough to sit at room temperature for 20 minutes, or until soft enough to form into balls. Preheat oven to 350 degrees. Form dough into 1 ½" balls, each weighing approximately 36 grams. Place on parchment-lined baking sheets 3" apart. Bake until slightly browned on edges and just slightly underdone in the middle, 15–18 minutes, rotating the pan halfway through baking. Leave the cookies on the baking sheet to cool for 10 minutes to set, and then transfer cookies to a wire rack to finish cooling. Store cookies in an airtight container for up to 2 weeks. Makes 4 dozen cookies.

YUMMIES AND PORTABLES

This section includes a number of cookie and treat recipes as well, but in this case they are from my and Phil's kitchen—and our hearts.

SPROUTED TAMARI ALMONDS

2 pounds raw almonds

Sunflower oil

Low-sodium tamari

These almonds go a long way toward getting me through the academic year. I leave them and a thermos of Organic India® Tulsi Chai Tea in the car for the long drive home, which, in the winter, can take as long as 90 minutes. Both these things combined keep me from swallowing the refrigerator once I arrive home.

Soak almonds covered in filtered water in the refrigerator overnight or for 6–8 hours. Drain well. Transfer almonds to a large bowl and sprinkle liberally with tamari, tossing with hands to distribute. Almonds should be coated but not oversaturated. Preheat oven to 200 degrees.

While almonds are resting, prepare as many cookie sheets as your oven will hold by spraying them with sunflower oil using a Misto® sprayer or by oiling using your hands or a paper towel. Spread almonds out in a single layer over the cookie sheets. Roast for 2 ½ hours or until crunchy. You can also dry them in a food dehydrator using the highest setting. Begin checking moisture content after 4 hours. Allow almonds to cool before transferring them to an air-tight storage container, where they'll keeps for several weeks. Makes 2 pounds.

G-MA'S HIKING MIX

Sprouted Tamari Almonds (see page 147)

Banana chips, slightly crushed

Juice-sweetened dried cranberries

Raw cashews

Raw pumpkin seeds

Dried pineapple chunks

This treat is necessary for all camping and road trips. I like it best with organic fruit we dry ourselves. The intersection of the slightly salty taste of Sprouted Tamari Almonds and the sweet fruit is quite satisfying. By the way, if you buy dried pineapple, it's less expensive to buy it in rings and chop it yourself.

Mix together equal amounts of nuts, seeds, and fruits. Store well-sealed in a cool, dark place.

CHERRY POWER BALLS

½ cup fresh almond butter

½ cup Kirkland Signature™ peanut butter

¼ cup sunflower meal

¾ cup dried cherries

1 + 1 tablespoon coconut oil

1 tablespoon hemp powder

1 tablespoon coconut flour

2 tablespoons rice syrup

½ teaspoon salt

12 ounces Enjoy Life® Dark Chocolate Morsels

These have such a long story behind them. They started out 30 years ago as a recipe in *Laurel's Kitchen* and were a thing I made time and again for my sons. When Phil and I went vegetarian in 2010, I dug them out as a way to shore up our blood sugars and help with protein intake. We made them by the dozens to take to readings when *Blue Moon Vegetarian* came out. The version in that book is called "Protein Balls." One day I didn't have most of the ingredients, so I worked with what I had on hand, and something completely new was born. The book's photographer, Suzi Hathaway, kept calling them "Power Balls" on the day we were shooting them—so many times that I declared that must be their new name. The cherries' brightness is quite unexpected, and they are so satisfying that one is all it takes.

Process the first 9 ingredients (but only 1 tablespoon of the coconut oil) in a food processor until very smooth and well-blended. Shape into 1" balls. Moisten hands as needed with coconut oil to keep from sticking. Melt chocolate and remaining coconut oil in a small pan over low heat and combine. Dip balls into mixture and set on a plate lined with parchment paper. Cool in the refrigerator until set up. Stores nicely in refrigerator for up to 2 weeks. Makes 3 dozen balls.

AGAVE CARAMEL CORN

½ cup organic popcorn kernels

3 tablespoons coconut oil

¼ cup agave syrup

¼ cup organic cane sugar

½ cup vegan butter

½ teaspoon baking soda

Once you have cooked organic popcorn on top of the stove in coconut oil, you never go back—and once you've tried this caramel corn, you'll be ruined for any other.

Preheat oven to 300 degrees. Butter two cookie sheets. Place coconut oil and several corn kernels into a heavy-bottomed kettle on stovetop on the highest setting. Heat until test kernels pop, and then add the rest of the popcorn and cover with lid. Shake pan by moving back and forth over heat until corn popping slows to a rate of 1 every 5 seconds. Be careful to wear oven mitts and to grip by the handles, since the pan will be very hot. Divide popped corn and place inside two sets of doubled (one inside the other), full-size brown paper grocery sacks and set aside.

In a medium-sized saucepan, heat agave syrup, sugar, and butter to a rolling boil and cook for 3–4 minutes. Turn off heat. **Be very careful since the hot agave mixture can cause severe burns.** Add baking soda to hot liquid and stir. The mixture will turn foamy. Drizzle ⅛ cup of the mixture at a time over the popped corn, intermittently closing the grocery sacks and shaking to distribute foam and coat corn evenly. Divide coated corn between the two baking sheets and spread out evenly. Bake for 3 minutes, and then remove from oven and stir. Return to oven for 3 more minutes, and then remove from oven and stir again. Repeat this process until corn is golden brown. Allow to cool before eating. Makes 3–4 servings.

ELEGANT DESSERT GORP

1 cup dried cherries

½ cup Enjoy Life® Semi-Sweet Chocolate Mega Chunks

1 cup raw almonds

Blue Moon Vegetarian includes quite a discussion about why I like Mariani® dried fruits. I've since fallen in love again with drying my own. Once you try Enjoy Life® chocolate (which is vegan and gluten-free), well, you won't go back.

Toast raw almonds at 225 degrees for 2 hours or until the skins just start to darken. Allow almonds to cool, and then chop very coarsely. Combine all ingredients thoroughly. Add extra chocolate chips if desired. Makes 10 ¼-cup servings.

INTERNATIONAL DAY OF HAPPINESS COOKIES

3 large, ripe bananas, well mashed (about 1 ½ cups)

1 teaspoon high-quality vanilla extract

½ cup coconut oil, melted but not hot

1 ¾ cups rolled oats, ground to flour

92 grams chickpea flour

¼ cup coconut sugar

¼ cup organic cane sugar

⅓ cup coconut, finely shredded and unsweetened

½ teaspoon high-quality ground cinnamon

1 teaspoon sea salt

1 teaspoon baking powder

¼ cup candied ginger, very finely chopped

5 dried apricots, very finely chopped

12 ounces Enjoy Life® Dark Chocolate Mini-Chips

Yes, Virginia, there is an International Day of Happiness, as declared by the U.N. See my website at www.PaulaMarieCoomer.com for further explanation. I kept these cookies separate from Jan's, mostly because they are such a different kind of cookie—they're more like a round granola bar than anything else, and I actually like them as a breakfast treat.

Preheat oven to 325 degrees, with racks set in the middle of the oven. In a large bowl combine the bananas, vanilla extract, and vegetable oil. Set aside. In another medium-sized bowl whisk together oats, almond flour, coconut sugar, shredded coconut, cinnamon, salt, and baking powder. Add dry ingredients to wet ingredients and stir until combined. Fold in ginger and chocolate chips. The dough will be somewhat loose. Drop a scant tablespoon at a time, 1" apart, onto parchment-lined baking sheet. Bake for 14–15 minutes, or as long as possible without burning the bottoms. Makes 4 dozen cookies.

GINGER NEWTONS

1 cup coconut oil

2 cups coconut sugar

½ cup molasses

2 teaspoons high-quality vanilla extract

248 grams sorghum flour

171 grams tapioca flour

74 grams potato starch

1 teaspoon xanthan gum

1 teaspoon baking soda

1 teaspoon sea salt

½ teaspoon ground cinnamon

Unsweetened coconut milk beverage

1 cup mixed raw nuts

1 cup candied ginger

¼ cup coconut sugar

½ cup vegan butter

These came out of my first attempt to make gluten-free gingersnaps. If you love ginger, they are definitely for you, but the ginger filling makes them a bit spicy, so children may turn up a nose. Perfect for holiday cookie swaps.

Preheat oven to 325 degrees. Line two 9" x 12" pans with parchment paper. In a large bowl, cream together coconut oil and sugar. Add vanilla and molasses. Mix until thoroughly combined. In a separate medium-sized bowl, mix dry ingredients. Sift into wet ingredients and blend until combined, conditioning with small amounts of coconut milk. Knead until a moldable dough forms. Divide dough in two and press into the bottom of each pan.

Process nuts and ginger with coconut sugar and vegan margarine in a food processor briefly until coarsely ground. Spread mixture over one of the prepared pans of dough. Press mixture into dough with hands or the back of a buttered wooden spoon.

Carefully invert the second pan (with parchment paper side up) and lower dough on top of the ginger and nut layer. The ginger and nut layer should be sandwiched between the two layers of dough. Press second dough layer firmly into ginger and nut layer, using the bottom of the second pan. Make sure the parchment paper remains between top dough layer and pan. The two dough layers should essentially be fused by the fruit/nut layer.

Remove the top pan and top parchment layer. Bake until toothpick inserted in the center comes out clean. Begin checking for doneness after 30 minutes. Allow to cool before cutting into bars. Wrap individually in wax paper and store in a closed container in the refrigerator, where the bars will keep for 2 weeks. Makes 2 dozen bars.

MILLION DOLLAR COOKIES

2 flax eggs (see page 24)

333 grams gluten-free oat flour

186 grams sorghum flour

1 teaspoon salt

1 teaspoon cardamom

1 teaspoon xanthan gum

1 teaspoon baking soda

2 teaspoon vanilla

1 cup coconut sugar

1 cup coconut oil

Unsweetened coconut milk beverage as needed

What a perfect way to end *Blue Moon Vegan*. This cookie is such a great example of the way Phil and I just happen to create recipes. It was one of those winter nights when we were craving a treat but didn't have much on hand. The recipe was simple but so good that Phil declared them "million dollar cookies." Enough said.

Prepare flax eggs and set aside. Preheat oven to 400 degrees. Mix all ingredients in a large bowl. Spoon batter onto greased baking sheet. Bake for 20 minutes. Makes 3 dozen cookies (if you don't eat too much of the raw dough).

WHERE TO BUY THINGS

Please note that I am not sponsored in any way by products or merchandisers. I am simply sharing my experience. Where specific brands have been mentioned, it is because that particular product works best in the recipe in terms of flavor or texture. Always, always experiment for yourself.

We buy most of our bulk items and other basic products such as toothpaste and shampoo through a whole foods buying club. Our supplier is Azure Standard in Dufur, Oregon, and they deliver in many states. Explore Azure at www.AzureStandard.com.

What we don't get through Azure, we buy locally through farmers markets, artisans (for soap, lotions, and lip balm), and especially our food co-op. When we travel, we make it a point to seek out these types of places and events to hunt for bargains, and when we find good prices, we stock up. For a list of co-ops near you, check out www.CoOpDirectory.org/.

The best place for herbs, spices, and great teas is Organic India®. Look for them at www.OrganicIndia.com. If I've mentioned an ingredient that you can't find at your local co-op or organic foods market, you can definitely find it there.

COOL, TRUSTWORTHY RESOURCES

This is a list of resources consulted in the writing of this book. As someone who teaches research and writing at a university, I've listed here only information from sources I trust. I believe it is important to educate yourself as much as possible about the workings of the body, which means I don't recommend taking my word for anything. Read for yourself. Get an anatomy coloring book and learn about organ systems. Read about basic physiology. Understand how your body functions and why good food is so important. Make taking care of your physical self your first priority. When you do that, it is pretty incredible how all other problems start falling away.

The China Study
- Campbell, T. Colin and Thomas M. Campbell, II. *The China Study: The Most Comprehensive Study of Nutrition Ever Conducted and the Startling Implications for Diet, Weight Loss and Long-Term Health*. Dallas, TX: Ben Bella Books, 2005.
- www.TheChinaStudy.com
- www.VegSource.com/news/2010/07/china-study-author-colin-campbell-slaps-down-critic-denise-minger.html

Hunger
- http://FeedingAmerica.org/hunger-in-america/hunger-facts/hunger-and-poverty-statistics.aspx
- https://apps.ams.usda.gov/fooddeserts/fooddeserts.aspx

The Relationship between Inflammation and Disease
- www.ncbi.nlm.nih.gov/pubmed/18240538
- www.NutritionandMetabolism.com/content/9/1/32
- www.Direct-MS.org/pdf/ImmunologyMS/Inflamm%20Neurodegen%20Review%2007.pdf
- www.Health.com/health/gallery/0,,20705881,00.html

Genetically Modified Foods
- www.Discovery.com/tv-shows/curiosity/topics/10-genetically-modified-food-products.htm
- www.csa.com/discoveryguides/gmfood/overview.php
- www.HuffingtonPost.com/2014/07/10/gmo-labels-congress_n_5576255.html

Coconut Oil
- www.WebMD.com/diet/features/coconut-oil-and-health?page=3
- http://Wakeup-World.com/2012/03/02/160-uses-for-coconut-oil/

Cooking Without Eggs
- www.TheSweetLifeOnline.com/2012/1/29/replacing-eggs/
- www.WellnessBakeries.com/egg-substitutes-2/
- www.OrganicAuthority.com/health/egg-substitutes-vegan-baking.html
- www.HerbWisdom.com/herb-psyllium-husk.html
- http://GlutenFreeGirl.com/2012/07/what-is-psyllium-husk/
- http://GlutenFreeGirl.com/2011/05/baking-without-eggs/

Xanthan and Guar Gums
- http://Gluten.LoveToKnow.com/xanthan-gum-substitute
- www.WebMD.com/vitamins-supplements/ingredientmono-919-GUAR%20GUM.aspx?activeIngredientId=919&activeIngredientName=GUAR%20GUM
- http://ChrisKresser.com/harmful-or-harmless-guar-gum-locust-bean-gum-and-more

Organic Certification
- http://tilth.org/

Films
- *Food, Inc.*
- *Forks Over Knives*
- *Future of Food*
- *Symphony of the Soil*
- *Two Angry Moms*
- *Vegucated*

VEGAN AND GLUTEN-FREE PROTEIN SOURCES

As long as you eat a varied diet, you really don't have to worry about getting enough protein, even if you are vegan. This little list hopefully gives you an idea why. Even a carrot has a gram of protein. To calculate your protein needs, follow this simple process:

- Record your desired body weight in pounds or kilograms: ____.

- If measured in pounds, multiply by 0.36 grams per day if you are in good health and in good physical condition.

- If measured in pounds and you are ill, pregnant, undergoing surgery, under stress, or engage in weight training, multiply by 0.6 grams per day.

- If measured in kilograms, multiply by 0.8 grams per day if you are in good health and in good physical condition.

- If measured in kilograms and you are ill, pregnant, undergoing surgery, under stress, or engage in weight training, multiply by 1.2 grams per day.

Protein Content in Common Vegan and Gluten-Free Foods

- Almonds—3 grams in 12 nuts
- Almond milk—2 grams in 1 cup
- Almond butter—2 grams in 1 tablespoon
- Apricots—1.5 grams in 3 medium-sized fruits
- Asparagus—3 grams in 1 ½ stalks
- Avocado—6 grams in one avocado with a 3 ½" diameter
- Bananas—1.5 grams in 1 medium-sized fruit
- Beets—2 grams in ¾ cup cooked
- Black beans—5.5 grams in ½ cup cooked
- Blackberries—1.5 grams in 1 cup
- Black-eyed peas—6.5 grams in ½ cup cooked
- Blueberries—1.5 grams in 1 cup
- Brown rice—2.5 grams in ½ cup cooked
- Brown rice flour—11 grams in 1 cup
- Buckwheat flour—11 grams in 1 cup
- Cabbage—2 grams in 1 cup cooked
- Carrot—1 gram in 1 large carrot
- Cashews—3 grams in 11 nuts
- Cauliflower—3 grams in 1 cup raw
- Celery—1 gram in 1 cup raw
- Chard—3 grams in 1 cup cooked
- Cherries—2 grams in 20 cherries
- Chickpeas—7 grams in ½ cup cooked
- Chickpea flour—6 grams in ¼ cup
- Chocolate (for baking)—4 grams in 1 ounce
- Coconut—2 grams in a 1" x 1" x 2" piece
- Collard greens—7 grams in 1 cup cooked
- Corn—3 grams in 1 cup cooked
- Cucumber—2 grams in 6 slices
- Dandelion greens—2 grams in 1 cup cooked
- Eggplant—2 grams in 1 cup cooked
- Green beans—2 grams in 1 cup cooked
- Hemp protein powder—9–15 grams in 3 tablespoons
- Kale—5 grams in 1 cup cooked
- Leeks—2 grams in 1 cup cooked
- Lentils—7 grams in ½ cup cooked
- Lettuce (all varieties)—1.5 grams in 2 cups chopped
- Lima beans—6 grams in ½ cup cooked
- Millet—1.5 grams in ½ cup cooked

- Miso—2 grams in 1 tablespoon
- Mustard greens—3 grams in 1 cup cooked
- Nutritional yeast—2.5 grams in 1 tablespoon
- Oats—3 grams in ½ cup cooked
- Oat milk—4 grams in 1 cup
- Okra—3 grams in 1 cup cooked
- Orange—1.5 grams in 1 medium-sized fruit
- Parsnips—2 grams in 1 cup cooked
- Peanuts—5 grams in 18 nuts
- Peanut butter—4 grams in 1 tablespoon
- Peas—8 grams in 1 cup cooked
- Pinto beans—7.3 grams in ½ cup cooked
- Pistachios—3.5 grams in 30 nuts
- Plums—3 grams in 3 medium-sized fruits
- Popcorn—1 gram in 1 cup popped
- Potatoes—4 grams in 4" x 2" baked potato
- Pumpkin—2 grams in 1 cup cooked
- Pumpkin seeds—5 grams in 2 tablespoons
- Quinoa—5 grams in ½ cup cooked
- Raisins—1.5 grams in ¼ cup
- Sorghum flour—16 grams in 1 cup
- Soybeans—11 grams in ½ cup cooked
- Spinach—4 grams in 2 cups raw
- Split peas—8 grams in ½ cup cooked
- Summer squash—2 grams in 1 cup cooked
- Sunflower butter—3 grams in 1 tablespoon
- Sunflower seeds—4 grams in 2 tablespoons
- Sweet potato—3 grams in 5" x 2" baked sweet potato
- Tangerine—2 grams in 3 medium-sized fruits
- Tempeh—11 grams in 2 ounces
- Tofu—9 grams in 2" x 2" x 1" piece
- Tomato—3 grams in 1 cup cooked
- Turnip—1.5 grams in 1 cup raw
- Walnuts—2 grams in 8 halves
- Watermelon—3 grams in 1" x 10" slice
- White beans—8 grams in ½ cup cooked
- Wild rice—4 grams in ½ cup cooked
- Winter squash—4 grams in 1 cup cooked
- Yellow split pea flour—11 grams in ¼ cup

Additional Sources of Protein for the Gluten-Tolerant

- Barley—3 grams in ½ cup cooked
- Rye flour—17 grams in 1 cup
- Whole wheat flour—16 grams in 1 cup
- Wheat flour (unbleached)—10 grams in 1 cup
- Wheat germ—1.5 grams in 1 tablespoon

Sources:

- Laurel Robertson, Carol Flinders, and Brian Ruppenthal. *The New Laurel's Kitchen*. Berkeley: Ten Speed Press, 1976.
- www.BobsRedMill.com

NOTE FROM PAULA MARIE COOMER

I hope you loved *Blue Moon Vegan* and are having a great time trying some of our yummy recipes. If you did, please take a moment to leave a review and rating on the online retailer of your choice. Reviews make it easier for other people to find good books and these days are like gold to authors.

Find out more about *Blue Moon Vegan* at www.paulamariecoomer.com/other-books-by-paula-marie-coomer/blue-moon-vegan/. And thank you so very much!

Subscribe to Receive My Rare and Occasional File Via Email

Please take a few moments to sign up for my Rare and Occasional File. From the title, you might have guessed that you won't be deluged with emails. But you will receive cool things I think are valuable enough to share, articles about writing and the writing life, about meatless and gluten-free living—including original recipes—and any other thing I think might enhance your living.

Not to mention a great little e-book for getting yourself down the path to more meatless meals. It's called "Going Vegetarian is not a Road, but a Highway" and it's free!

And signing up is super easy. Just go to www.paulamariecoomer.com/rare-and-occasional-file/. Looking forward to seeing you there!

Connect with me

You can reach me at **COOM1286@HOTMAIL.COM**.

TWITTER: @PMCoomer
FACEBOOK: www.facebook.com/paula.coomer.3
GOODREADS: www.goodreads.com/author/show/1018775.Paula_Marie_Coomer
WEBSITE: www.paulamariecoomer.com

INDEX

A

agar agar, as an egg substitute, 23
AGAVE CARAMEL CORN, 149
agave syrup:
    as a sweetener, 22
    AGAVE CARAMEL CORN, 149
alcohol:
    benefits of, 9
    and inflammation, 19
alder smoked sea salt, 31
alfredo sauce, vegan and gluten-free alternative, 104
allergies:
    and diet, 12
    misdiagnosis of, 14-15
    to wheat and gluten, 15-17
    to yeast, 33
almond flour, 43, 115
almond meal:
    baking with, 26-29
    in recipes, 47, 135, 141, 146
ALMONDS, SPROUTED TAMARI, 147-148
almonds:
    and gastrointestinal distress, 30
    as a source of protein, 160
    in recipes, 110, 147, 148, 150
    SPROUTED TAMARI ALMONDS, 147-148

ALMOST NIRVANA FRUIT SALAD, 60, 81
antibiotics:
    and health, 12, 14
    and probiotics, 96, 105
apples:
    and pesticide, 18
    in recipes, 45, 137
apple cider vinegar, as an egg substitute, 23
applesauce:
    as an egg substitute, 23
    how to make, 45
    in recipes, 45, 137-138
apricots:
    in recipes, 51, 151
    as a source of protein, 160
arrowroot:
    as a replacement for cornstarch 28
    in gluten-free baking, 28
    in recipes, 56, 100, 124-125
asparagus:
    and pesticide, 18
    as a source of protein, 160
    in recipe, 108
avocados:
    and pesticide, 18
    as a source of protein, 160

as an egg substitute, 23
in recipes, 56-57, 109, 112, 121, 126

B

BABY LENTIL STEW, 71, 82
BANANA-PEACH CRUNCH, 52
bananas:
    and pesticide, 18
    as a source of protein, 160
    as an egg substitute, 23
    chips, in recipe, 148
    in recipes, 35-36, 45, 48, 52, 60, 148, 151
barley, and gluten intolerance, 14
basil, 55-56, 59, 69-70, 72-74, 103, 106, 114, 116-118, 133
BASIL CASSEROLE, HOT TOMATO-, 84, 103
BASIL-GRAPEFRUIT VINAIGRETTE, 55, 79
basmati rice:
    about, 31
    in recipes, 57, 99, 101-103, 108, 111, 116, 121, 124-125
BEAN BOWL, IN-A-PINCH, 126
BEAN BURGERS, NUTTY BLACK, 110
BEAN BURRITOS, RED-HOT, FOUR-STAR, TWO-, 89, 121
BEAN CHEESY SPOONBREAD, THREE-, 115
BEAN CURRIED BISQUE, TWO-, 72
BEAN NACHOS, PHIL'S FABULOUS THREE-, 87, 112
BEAN SANDWICH SPREAD, FIVE-, 65
BEAN STEW, SPICY CHILI, 69
beans: see also *black beans, chickpeas, kidney beans, great northern beans, navy beans, pinto beans, red beans*
    as a source of protein, 160-161
    FIVE-BEAN SANDWICH SPREAD, 65
    FIVE BEANS, 65, 74, 109, 126
    fresh-cooked vs. canned, 72
    in the pantry, 30
    in recipes, 57, 65, 69, 72, 74, 83, 100, 109, 110, 112, 115, 116, 121-122, 126-127
    IN-A-PINCH BEAN BOWL, 126
    NUTTY BLACK BEAN BURGERS, 110
    PHIL'S FABULOUS THREE-BEAN NACHOS, 87, 112
    PHIL'S INFAMOUS BAKED BEANS, 100
    RED-HOT, FOUR-STAR, TWO-BEAN BURRITOS, 121
    SPICY CHILI BEAN STEW, 69
    THREE-BEAN CHEESY SPOONBREAD, 115
    TWO-BEAN CURRIED BISQUE, 72
BEANS, FIVE, 65, 74, 109, 126
BEANS, PHIL'S INFAMOUS BAKED, 83, 100
beets:
    and inflammation, 19
    and white sugar, 22, 31
    as a source of protein, 160
    BLOODROOT STEW WITH GRILLED SUNFLOWER SANDWICHES, 119
berries: see also *cranberries, huckleberries, strawberries*
    and inflammation, 19
    and pesticide, 18
    as a source of protein, 160
    in recipes, 35, 40, 60, 67, 148
BISCUITS AND GRAVY, BLUE MOON, 43-44, 78
BISQUE, TWO-BEAN CURRIED, 72
black beans:
    as a source of protein, 160
    in recipes, 100, 109-110, 112, 115-116, 121
black-eyed peas:
    as a source of protein, 160
    EXOTIC BLACK-EYED CHILI, 73
BLOODROOT STEW WITH GRILLED SUNFLOWER SANDWICHES, 119
blueberries:
    and pesticide, 18
    as a source of protein, 160
    BLUEBERRY-GINGER FIZZ, 40
BLUEBERRY-GINGER FIZZ, 40
BLUE MOON BISCUITS AND GRAVY, 43-44, 78

bok choy:
    in recipes, 55, 68, 79, 116, 118
        ENDIVE AND BOK CHOY IN CREAMY BASIL-GRAPEFRUIT VINAIGRETTE, 55, 79
BOK CHOY IN CREAMY BASIL-GRAPEFRUIT VINAIGRETTE, ENDIVE AND, 55, 79
BOULE, CRUSTY, 134-135
BOULE, RAISIN FENNEL, 135
BOULE, ROSEMARY WALNUT, 135
bread:
    baking gluten-free, 26-29
    CARAMELIZED ONION FOCACCIA, 133
    CRUSTY BOULE, 134-135
    egg substitutes for baking, 23-25
    FOCACCIA, 132-133
    GRANDMA'S 21ST CENTURY PANBREAD, 82, 97
    HONEY OAT SANDWICH BREAD, 90, 130-131
    in recipes, 49, 62-65, 119
    RAISIN FENNEL BOULE, 135
    ROASTED GARLIC FOCACCIA, 133
    ROSEMARY WALNUT BOULE, 135
    SUN-DRIED TOMATO FOCACCIA, 133
    THREE-BEAN CHEESY SPOONBREAD, 115
    WHITE SANDWICH BREAD, 89, 129-130
BREAD, HONEY OAT SANDWICH, 90, 130-131
BREAD, WHITE SANDWICH, 89, 129-130
brown rice flour:
    as a source of protein, 160
    baking with, 26-29
    in recipes, 48, 123, 139, 141
BRUNCH FLORENTINE, 49
BUNS, BURGER, 110, 113, 120, 131-132
BURGER BUNS, 110, 113, 120, 131-132
BURGERS, EVERYDAY GRILLING, 85, 122
BURGERS, IMPOSSIBLE, 113
BURGERS, NUTTY BLACK BEAN, 110
BURGERS, OAT-WALNUT, 120, 127
BURRITOS, EAST MEETS WEST, 88, 116
BURRITOS, RED-HOT, FOUR-STAR, TWO-BEAN, 89, 121

BUTTER-DILL SALAD, 56

C

cabbage:
    green, in recipe, 54
    red, in recipes, 53-54, 57, 61, 108
    as a source of protein, 160
CAKE, CARROT, 139
CAKE, CHERRY OAT SUNDAY, 23, 45
CAKE, CHOCOLATE, 91, 140
capers, 62, 65
CAN'T BE CHEESE, 49, 61, 65, 70, 95-96, 112
CARAMEL CORN, AGAVE, 149
CARAMELIZED ONION FOCACCIA, 133
CARROT CAKE, 139
CARROT PINEAPPLE COCONUT MUFFINS, 128
carrots:
    as a source of protein, 160
    CARROT CAKE, 139
    CARROT PINEAPPLE COCONUT MUFFINS, 128
    in recipes, 53-54, 61, 68, 70-71, 106, 110-111, 117, 119, 126, 137-139
CASHEW CREAM, SQUASH BLOSSOMS IN, 105
cashews:
    as a source of protein, 160
    as an egg yolk substitute, 24
    in recipes, 95-96, 105, 108, 125-126, 148
    making cheese from, 95-96
    SQUASH BLOSSOMS IN CASHEW CREAM, 105
CASSEROLE, HOT-TOMATO BASIL, 84, 103
cauliflower:
    and pesticide, 18,
    as a source of protein, 160
    in recipe, 104
CAULIFREDO, FETTUCINE, 104
celery:
    as a source of protein, 160
    in recipes, 58-59, 61, 63, 71, 73, 101, 111, 118, 126, 160
celiac disease, vs. gluten intolerance, 14

CHAI, CHOCOLATE SMOOTHIE, 36, 75
chard:
    as a source of protein, 160
    CHARD SUMMER SOUP, 67
CHARD SUMMER SOUP, 67
cheddar, vegan, 49, 57, 69, 112, 116, 118; see also *cheese*
CHEESE, CAN'T BE, 49, 61, 65, 70, 95-96, 112
cheese, vegan: see also *cheddar, feta, Monterey Jack, mozzarella*
    and probiotics, 105,
    CAN'T BE CHEESE, 49, 61, 65, 70, 95-96, 112
    flavor with nutritional yeast, 33
    in recipes, 49, 61, 65, 112-113, 115
CHERRY OAT SUNDAY CAKE, 23, 45
CHERRY POWER BALLS, 94, 148
cherries:
    and inflammation, 19
    and pesticide, 18
    as a source of protein, 160
    CHERRY OAT SUNDAY CAKE, 23, 45
    CHERRY POWER BALLS, 94, 148
    dried, 148, 150
chia seeds, as an egg substitute, 23-25
CHICK SALAD, 63
chickpea flour:
    as a source of protein, 160
    as an egg substitute, 24
    in recipes, 43, 47-48, 68, 96, 120
chickpeas:
    as a source of protein, 160
    CHICK SALAD, 63
    in recipes, 63, 98
CHILI BEAN STEW, SPICY, 69
CHILI, EXOTIC BLACK-EYED, 73
chocolate:
    as a source of protein, 160
    CHOCOLATE CAKE, 91, 140
    CHOCOLATE CHAI SMOOTHIE, 36, 75
    in recipes, 36-37, 60, 69, 73, 75, 91, 93, 140, 144-146, 148, 150, 151

CHOCOLATE CAKE, 91, 140
CHOCOLATE CHAI SMOOTHIE, 36, 75
CHOCOLATE CHIP COOKIES, 93, 146
CINNAMON ROLLS, 141-142
cocktails, 39, 40
COCONUT MACAROONS, 92, 144-145
coconut milk:
    as an egg yolk substitute, 24
    TOASTEDCOCONUTMOCHAFRAPPUCINO, 37, 76
COCONUT MUFFINS, CARROT PINEAPPLE, 138
coconut oil, benefits of, 25-26, 43, 158
coffee, 43-44, 140
COLESLAW, WESTERN, 53
cookies:
    baking with egg substitutes, 23
    CHOCOLATE CHIP COOKIES, 93, 146
    COCONUT MACAROONS, 92, 144-145
    GINGER NEWTONS, 152
    INTERNATIONAL DAY OF HAPPINESS COOKIES, 94, 151
    MILLION DOLLAR COOKIES, 153
    PEANUT BUTTER COOKIES, 92, 145-146
    recipe for, 92-94, 107, 116, 144-147, 149, 151-153
COOKIES, CHOCOLATE CHIP, 93,146
COOKIES, INTERNATIONAL DAY OF HAPPINESS, 94, 151
COOKIES, MILLION DOLLAR, 153
COOKIES, PEANUT BUTTER, 92, 145-146
corn:
    and pesticide: 18
    and xanthan gum, 22
    AGAVE CARAMEL CORN, 149
    as a source of protein, 160
    choosing organic, 18, 22
    flour in gluten-free baking, 28
cornmeal, 97, 115, 143
cornstarch, in gluten-free baking, 28-29
CRACKERS, "GRAHAM", 91, 143-144
cranberries, 148

CRUST, PIZZA, 135-136
CRUSTY BOULE, 134-135
cucumbers:
    as a source of protein, 160
    in recipes, 61, 126
cupcakes, 139-140
CURRIED, TWO-BEAN BISQUE, 72

D

dairy:
    and inflammation, 19
    detox from, 12
    nondairy alternatives to milk, 129
DAY AT THE BEACH, 39, 77
DESSERT GORP, ELEGANT, 150
DILL SALAD, BUTTER-, 56
Dirty Baker's Dozen, 17-18
DISAPPEARING KALE SLAW, 54

E

EAST MEETS WEST BURRITOS, 55, 88, 116
EGG SALAD, HIPPIE, 62
eggplant:
    as a source of protein, 160
    in recipe, 99
eggs:
    cooking without, 158
    substitutes in vegan baking, 22-25,
    HIPPIE EGG SALAD, 62
ELEGANT DESSERT GORP, 150
ENDIVE AND BOK CHOY IN CREAMY BASIL-
    GRAPEFRUIT VINAIGRETTE, 55, 79
endive, 55, 79, 116
Ener-G® Egg Replacer™, about, 24
EVERYDAY GRILLING BURGERS, 85, 122
EXOTIC BLACK-EYED CHILI, 73

F

feta, tofu, 114
FETTUCCINE CAULIFREDO, 104

FIVE BEANS, 65, 74, 109, 126
FIVE-BEAN SANDWICH SPREAD, 65
flax seed, as an egg substitute, 23-25
flours: see also *almond flour, almond meal, brown rice flour, chickpea flour, millet flour, oat flour, rice flour, sorghum flour, white rice flour*
    as a source of protein, 160-162
    baking with gluten-free, 15-17, 26-29
    creating your own blends, 27-29
    weighing, 26-29
FOCACCIA, 132-133
FOCACCIA, SUN-DRIED TOMATO, 133
FOCACCIA, CARAMELIZED ONION, 133
FOCACCIA, ROASTED GARLIC, 133
FRAGRANT PANCAKES, 48
FRIES, SUZI'S BAKED HOME, 85, 107
frosting, buttercream, 139
FRUIT SALAD, ALMOST NIRVANA, 60, 81
fruits: see also *apples, applesauce, apricots, bananas, berries, blueberries, cranberries, grapefruit, huckleberries, lemons, mangoes, nectarines, oranges, peaches, pumpkin, strawberries*
    ALMOST NIRVANA FRUIT SALAD, 60, 81
    and inflammation, 18-19
    and pesticide, 17-18
    as a source of protein, 160-161
    as an egg substitute, 23
    genetically modified, 20
    in recipes, 35-36, 39-41, 45, 48, 50-52, 55-56, 59-60, 65, 67, 72, 95, 105, 114, 116, 137-138, 148, 150-151
FUZZY TEA, 38

G

garbanzo beans: see *chickpeas*
GARDEN LENTIL SOUP, 68
GARLIC FOCACCIA, ROASTED, 133
garlic:
    and inflammation, 19,
    ROASTED GARLIC FOCACCIA, 133

in recipes, 43-44, 46, 49, 54, 59, 68-74, 98-101, 103-104, 106-110, 112, 114-119, 121-122, 125-126, 133
gelatin, as a binder, 23
genetically modified foods, about, 20, 158
ginger:
   and inflammation, 19
   BLUEBERRY-GINGER FIZZ, 40
   candied, 40, 51, 60, 151-152
   GINGER NEWTONS, 152
   GINGERY RICE, 84, 101
   in recipes, 40, 51, 54, 60, 99, 101, 108, 111, 125, 138, 151-152
GINGER NEWTONS, 152
GINGERY RICE, 84, 101
gluten:
   and inflammation, 19
   intolerance, 14-16
gluten-free:
   baking, 15-16, 26-29
   benefits, 13-16
   flour: see *flours*
   sources of protein, 160-162
G-MA'S HIKING MIX, 148
GMOs, see *genetically modified foods*
GORP, ELEGANT DESSERT, 150
GOULASH, SPICY, 118
"GRAHAM" CRACKERS, 91, 143-144
grains:
   and gluten-free baking, 26-29
   and inflammation, 19
GRANDMA'S 21ST CENTURY PANBREAD, 82, 97
GRANOLA, PAULA'S VERSION OF THE WORLD'S BEST, 51-52, 79
granola, 51-52, 79
grapefruits:
   candied, 55
   in recipes, 39, 55-56, 116
   BASIL-GRAPEFRUIT VINAIGRETTE, 55, 79
GRAPEFRUIT VINAIGRETTE, BASIL-, 55, 79

GRAVY, BLUE MOON BISCUITS AND, 43-44, 78
GRAVY, RED-EYE, 44
GREAT (E)SCAPE VICHYSSOISE, 68
great northern beans, 100
greens: see also *lettuce, romaine*
   and inflammation, 19
   as a source of protein, 160-161
   in recipes, 109, 126
GREEN BEANS, PHIL'S HOT AND SPICY STIR-FRIED, 86, 107
green onions, 54, 59
GRILLED VEGETABLE POLOU, 83, 99
GRILLING BURGERS, EVERYDAY, 85, 122
guacamole, 112
guar gum:
   about, 22-23, 158
   as an egg substitute, 24

H

hamburger: see *burgers*
hazelnuts, 59
HEMP, 35
hemp:
   as a source of protein, 160
   benefits of, 30, 32
   in recipes, 35, 47, 69, 74, 123, 127, 148
   PHIL'S DAILY HEMP SHAKE, 13, 35
herbs, shopping for, 31, 155
HERBED FRENCH LENTIL SOUP, 70
HIKING MIX, G-MA'S, 148
HIPPIE EGG SALAD, 62
honey, and veganism, 21-22
HONEY OAT SANDWICH BREAD, 90, 130-131
HOT TOMATO-BASIL CASSEROLE, 84, 103
huckleberries, 60
HUMMUS, MOST HONORABLE, 98

I

ICEBOX SOUP, 74, 109
IMPOSSIBLE BURGERS, 113

IN-A-PINCH BEAN BOWL, 126
inflammation, and diet, 13, 18-19, 32, 158
INTERNATIONAL DAY OF HAPPINESS
  COOKIES, 94, 151

J
jalapeño peppers, 112, 116
jicama, 121, 126

K
kale:
  and inflammation, 19
  as a source of protein, 160
  DISAPPEARING KALE SLAW, 54
KALE SLAW, DISAPPEARING, 54
kebobs, 99
kidney beans, 57, 100, 109, 112, 115

L
lard, and inflammation, 19
LASAGNA AL FORNO, PAULA'S, 88, 117
LAVENDER DREAM, MALLORY'S, 42
leeks:
  as a source of protein, 160
  in recipes, 57, 67, 101, 111, 118, 126
lemons, 40-41, 59-60, 72, 95, 105, 114
LENTIL POLOU, SWEET, 102, 118
LENTIL SOUP, GARDEN, 68
LENTIL SOUP, HERBED FRENCH, 70
LENTIL STEW, BABY, 71, 82
lentils:
  as a source of protein, 160
  BABY LENTIL STEW, 71, 82
  GARDEN LENTIL SOUP, 68
  HERBED FRENCH LENTIL SOUP, 70
  in recipes, 68, 70-71, 102, 109, 118, 123, 160
  SWEET LENTIL POLOU, 102, 118
lettuce: see also *greens, romaine*
  as a source of protein, 160
  in recipes, 55-57, 61-65, 113, 126

lime, juice of, 39, 60, 112, 125
linguini, 105
LOTUS TOFU IN SWEET SESAME SAUCE, 124

M
MACAROONS, COCONUT, 92, 144-145
MALLORY'S LAVENDER DREAM, 42
mangoes: see also *fruits*
  and pesticide, 18
  in recipe, 35
marinade, tempeh, 64
MEAT LOAF, NOT, 123, 127
meat, and inflammation, 19
MIGHTY FINE TACO SALAD, 57
millet flour, 48, 141
MILLION DOLLAR COOKIES, 153
Monterey Jack cheese, vegan, 119, 121
MORNING GLORY MUFFINS, 137
MOST HONORABLE HUMMUS, 98
mozzarella, vegan, 117
muffins:
  CARROT CAKE MUFFINS, 139
  CARROT PINEAPPLE COCONUT MUFFINS, 138
  CHOCOLATE CAKE MUFFINS, 91, 140
  egg substitutes for baking 23-25
  baking gluten-free, 26-29
  MORNING GLORY MUFFINS, 137
  ORANGE ZUCCHINI MUFFINS, 90, 138
  PUMPKIN SPICE MUFFINS, 138

N
NACHOS, PHIL'S FABULOUS THREE-BEAN, 87, 112
navy beans, 72, 109
nectarines:
  and pesticide, 18
  in recipe, 60
NEW KENTUCKY POTATO SALAD, 58, 80
noodles: see *pasta*

NOT MEAT LOAF, 123, 127
nuts: see also *almonds, cashews, hazelnuts, peanuts, pine nuts, walnuts*
    about, 30
    and inflammation, 19
    and pesticide, 18
    as a source of protein, 160-161
    in recipes, 51-52, 59-61, 74, 95-96, 102, 105, 108, 110, 114, 117, 120, 122-123, 125-127, 135, 137-139, 145, 147-148, 150, 152
nutrition, and metabolism, 158
nutritional yeast:
    about, 33
    as a source of protein, 161
NUTTY BLACK BEAN BURGERS, 110

O

oat flour:
    baking with, 26-29
    in recipes, 47, 115, 134, 153
OAT SUNDAY CAKE, CHERRY, 23, 45
OAT-WALNUT BURGERS, 120, 127
OATMEAL -WALNUT LOAF, 127
oats:
    as a source of protein, 161
    choosing gluten-free, 31
    CHERRY OAT SUNDAY CAKE, 23, 45
    HONEY OAT SANDWICH BREAD, 90, 130-131
    in recipes, 45, 51, 110, 113, 122, 151
    OAT-WALNUT BURGERS, 120
    OATMEAL-WALNUT LOAF, 127
oil, about, 29-30
olive oil, and inflammation, 19
olives, 65
ONION FOCACCIA, CARAMELIZED, 133
onions:
    and inflammation, 19
    and pesticide, 18
    CARAMELIZED ONION FOCACCIA, 133
    in recipes, 57-58, 62-63, 68-73, 98-100, 102-104, 106, 108-110, 113-114, 116-117, 119-123, 126, 133
ORANGE ZUCCHINI MUFFINS, 90, 138
oranges:
    as a source of protein, 161
    in recipe, 59, 65, 138
organic foods:
    and GMOs, 20, 22
    benefits of, 17-18
    cane sugar, 22, 31
    certification, 158
    soy, 32

P

pancakes:
    egg substitutes for, 23-25
    FRAGRANT PANCAKES, 48
    recipes for, 47-48
    SKILLET CAKES, 47
PANCAKES, FRAGRANT, 48
pastas:
    in recipes, 59, 104-105, 114
    SUNNY PASTA SALAD, 59, 80
PASTA SALAD, SUNNY, 59, 80
pastries:
    egg substitutes for, 23-25
    recipes for, 141-142
PAULA'S LASAGNA AL FORNO, 88, 117
PAULA'S VERSION OF THE WORLD'S BEST GRANOLA, 51-52, 79
PEACH CRUNCH, BANANA, 52
PEACH PERSUASION, VIOLET-, 41
peaches:
    and pesticide, 18
    BANANA-PEACH CRUNCH, 52
    in recipes, 41, 52
    VIOLET-PEACH PERSUASION, 41
PEANUT BUTTER COOKIES, 92, 145-146
peanut butter:
    as a source of protein, 161

in recipes, 73, 145, 148
PEANUT BUTTER COOKIES, 92, 145
peanuts:
   and inflammation, 19
   as a source of protein, 161
   in recipe, 145
peppers, bell:
   and inflammation, 19
   and pesticide, 18
   in recipes, 46, 53, 59, 62-63, 65, 69, 99-101, 106, 108, 114, 117-118, 121
pesticides, about, 17-18, 31
PHIL'S DAILY HEMP SHAKE, 13, 35
PHIL'S FABULOUS THREE-BEAN NACHOS, 87, 112
PHIL'S HOT AND SPICY STIR-FRIED GREEN BEANS, 86, 107
PHIL'S INFAMOUS BAKED BEANS, 83, 100
PHIL'S MELLOW YELLOW SCRAMBLE, 46
PHIL'S VEGETABLE ROLL-UPS, 61, 81, 96
PHIL'S WEST TEXAS GREEK COMPANY SUPPER, 87, 114
pine nuts, 74, 102, 114
PINEAPPLE COCONUT MUFFINS, CARROT, 138
pineapples:
   and pesticide, 18
   CARROT PINEAPPLE COCONUT MUFFINS, 138
   in recipes, 60, 138, 148
pinto beans:
   as a source of protein, 161
   in recipes, 72, 112, 115-116, 121
PIZZA CRUST, 135-136
POLOU, GRILLED VEGETABLE, 83, 99
POLOU, SWEET LENTIL, 102 118
popcorn:
   as a source of protein, 161
   AGAVE CARAMEL CORN, 149
potato flour:
   baking with, 26-29
   in recipe, 45

potatoes:
   and pesticide, 18
   as a source of protein, 161
   NEW KENTUCKY POTATO SALAD, 58, 80
   in recipes, 58, 68, 71, 119
   SUZY'S BAKED HOME FRIES, 107
POTATO SALAD, NEW KENTUCKY, 58, 80
probiotics, 95-96, 105
PROTEIN, 159
protein:
   animal, and inflammation, 13
   hemp, 32
   vegan and gluten-free sources of, 159-162
psyllium husk, about, 25
PUDDING, PUMPKIN, 50
pumpkin:
   as an egg substitute, 23
   as a source of protein, 161
   in recipes, 50
   PUMPKIN PUDDING, 50
   PUMPKIN SPICE MUFFINS, 138
PUMPKIN PUDDING, 50
pumpkin seeds:
   as a source of protein, 161
   in recipes, 54, 113, 148,
PUMPKIN SPICE MUFFINS, 138

Q

quinoa:
   about, 13
   as a source of protein, 161
   in recipe, 59

R

radishes, 56
RAISIN FENNEL BOULE, 135
raisins:
   as a source of protein, 161
   in recipes, 135, 137-138
   RAISIN FENNEL BOULE, 135

red beans, 69, 109
RED-EYE GRAVY, 44
RED-HOT, FOUR-STAR, TWO-BEAN BURRITOS, 89, 121
RICE BOWL WITH ASIAN EVERYTHING SAUCE, 125
rice flour, sweet: see also *brown rice flour, white rice flour*
    baking with, 26-29
    in recipes, 131, 138-139, 141, 143
RICE, GINGERY, 84, 101
RICE, TESLA'S, 111, 118
rice:
    as a source of protein, 160-161
    GINGERY RICE, 84, 101
    in recipes, 57, 74, 99, 101-103, 108, 111, 116, 118, 121, 124-125
    RICE BOWL WITH ASIAN EVERYTHING SAUCE, 125
    TESLA'S RICE, 111, 118
ROASTED GARLIC FOCACCIA, 133
ROLLS, CINNAMON, 141-142
romaine, 57; see also *greens, lettuce*
ROSEMARY WALNUT BOULE, 135

S

SALAD, ALMOST NIRVANA FRUIT, 60, 81
SALAD, BUTTER-DILL, 56
SALAD, CHICK, 63
SALAD, HIPPIE EGG, 62
SALAD, MIGHTY FINE TACO, 57
SALAD, NEW KENTUCKY POTATO, 58, 80
SALAD, SUNNY PASTA, 59, 80
salads, 53-60, 62-63, 126
SANDWICH BREAD, HONEY OAT, 90, 130-131
SANDWICH BREAD, WHITE, 89, 129-130
SANDWICH, GRILLED SUNFLOWER, 119
SANDWICH SPREAD, FIVE-BEAN, 65
sandwiches, 61-65, 119
SANDWICHES, GRILLED SUNFLOWER, 119
SAUCE, LOTUS TOFU IN SWEET SESAME, 124
SAUCE, RICE BOWL WITH ASIAN EVERYTHING, 125
SAUCE, TOMATO, 85, 106
sauce, 104, 106, 117, 124-125
scapes, 68
serrano peppers, 73
SKILLET CAKES, 47, 78
SLAW, DISAPPEARING KALE, 54
SMOOTHIE, CHOCOLATE CHAI, 36, 75
smoothies, 35-36
sorghum flour:
    as a source of protein, 161
    baking with, 26-29
    in recipes, 45, 141-142, 146, 152-153
SOUP, CHARD SUMMER, 67
SOUP, GARDEN LENTIL, 68
SOUP, HERBED FRENCH LENTIL, 70
SOUP, ICEBOX, 74, 109
soups, 67-74, 109
soy: see *tofu*
soybeans:
    choosing organic, 18, 32
    as a source of protein, 161
SPICY CHILI BEAN STEW, 69
SPICY GOULASH, 118
SPICY TLT ON TOAST, 64
spinach:
    and inflammation, 19
    and pesticide 18,
    as a source of protein, 161
    in recipes, 35, 49, 117
SPOONBREAD, THREE-BEAN CHEESY, 115
SPRING FEVER, 86, 108
SPROUTED TAMARI ALMONDS, 147-148
starches, in gluten-free baking, 27-29
STEW, BABY LENTIL, 71, 82
STEW, BLOODROOT, 119
STEW, SPICY CHILI BEAN, 69
strawberries:
    and pesticide, 18
    in recipe, 67

SQUASH BLOSSOMS IN CASHEW CREAM, 105
squash, yellow: see *yellow squash*
squash, winter: see *winter squash*
sugar, choosing organic, 22, 31
SUN-DRIED TOMATO FOCACCIA, 133
SUNFLOWER SANDWICHES, GRILLED, 119
sunflower seeds:
    as a source of protein, 161
    in recipes, 110, 123, 126
SUNNY PASTA SALAD, 59, 80
SURPRISING TORTILLAS, 61, 96, 116, 121
SUZI'S BAKED HOME FRIES, 85, 107
SWEET LENTIL POLOU, 102, 118
Sweeteners:
    vegan and gluten-free, 21-22
    synthetic, and inflammation, 19

T

TACO SALAD, MIGHTY FINE, 57
tapioca flour:
    baking with, 26-29
    in recipes, 45, 115
tempeh:
    about, 33
    as a source of protein, 161
    in recipes, 64, 125
    marinade for, 64
    SPICY TLT ON TOAST, 64
tequila, 39, 42
TESLA'S RICE, 111, 118
THREE-BEAN CHEESY SPOONBREAD, 115
TOASTED COCONUT MOCHA FRAPPUCINO, 37, 76
TOFU IN SWEET SESAME SAUCE, LOTUS, 124
tofu:
    and inflammation, 19
    as a source of protein, 161
    as an egg substitute, 25
    choosing organic, 32
    in recipes, 46, 49-50, 62, 111, 113-114, 117, 124
    preparation of, 32

TOMATO-BASIL CASSEROLE, HOT, 84, 103
TOMATO FOCACCIA, SUN-DRIED, 133
TOMATO SAUCE, 85, 106
tomatoes:
    and inflammation, 19
    as a source of protein, 161
    green, 67
    HOT TOMATO-BASIL CASSEROLE, 84, 103
    in recipes, 57, 64-65, 67, 69, 73-74, 99, 103, 113, 114, 117, 126
    yellow, 65
TORTILLAS, SURPRISING, 61, 96, 116, 121
TWO-BEAN CURRIED BISQUE, 72

V

VEGAN, 12, 159
Vegan diet:
    and sweeteners, 21-22
    benefits of, 11-13
    and cheese: see *cheese*
    egg substitutes, 22-25, 158
VEGETABLE POLOU, GRILLED, 83, 99
VEGETABLE ROLL-UPS, PHIL'S, 61, 81, 96
vegetables: see also *asparagus, beets, black-eyed peas, bok choy, cabbage, carrots, cauliflower, celery, chard, corn, cucumber, eggplant, endive, greens, green beans, green onions, jalapeño peppers, jicama, kale, leeks, lettuce, onions, peppers, potatoes, radishes, romaine, serrano peppers, squash, spinach, tomatoes, winter squash*
    and inflammation, 18-19
    and pesticide, 17-18
    as a source of protein, 160-161
    as an egg substitute, 23
    genetically modified, 20
    GRILLED VEGETABLE POLOU, 83, 99
    in recipes, 46, 49, 53-59, 61-65, 67-74, 98-114, 116-123, 125-126, 128, 133, 138-139
    PHIL'S VEGETABLE ROLL-UPS, 61, 81, 96
VICHYSSOISE, GREAT (E)SCAPE, 68

VINAIGRETTE, BASIL-GRAPEFRUIT, 55, 79, 116
VIOLET-PEACH PERSUASION, 41
violets, candied, 41
vitamin deficiencies, 13-14

W
WALNUT BOULE, ROSEMARY, 135
WALNUT BURGERS, OAT-, 120, 127
WALNUT LOAF, OATMEAL-, 127
walnuts: see also *nuts*
    as a source of protein, 161
    in recipes, 60-61, 117, 120, 123, 127, 135, 137-139
WESTERN COLESLAW, 53
wheat: see *gluten*
white rice flour:
    baking with, 26-29
    in recipes, 43-44, 47-48, 67, 96-97, 113
WHITE SANDWICH BREAD, 89, 129-130
winter squash:
    as a source of protein, 161
    in recipes, 46, 114

X
xanthan gum:
    about, 22, 158
    as an egg substitute, 25

Y
yeast, nutritional: see *nutritional yeast*
yellow squash, 103

Z
ziti, 114
zucchini:
    ORANGE ZUCCHINI MUFFINS, 90, 138
    in recipes, 108, 114, 138
ZUCCHINI MUFFINS, ORANGE, 90, 138

PRAISE FOR PAULA MARIE COOMER'S PREVIOUS WORK

Blue Moon Vegetarian

Blue Moon Vegetarian is a book that will feed all the essential parts of you: your body, your mind, your soul. It's a love story, a health journal, a cookbook, a lyrical memoir—the perfect recipe for anyone who desires to live a deliciously examined life.
—Kim Barnes, author of the internationally-acclaimed novel *In the Kingdom of Men*

WWW.PAULAMARIECOOMER.COM/OTHER-BOOKS-BY-PAULA-MARIE-COOMER/
BLUE-MOON-VEGETARIAN/

Dove Creek

Dove Creek is a wise, eloquent, fiercely honest fictional chronicle. Paula Marie Coomer writes like a house afire, and her richly variegated novel deserves a prominent place in the literature of the modern American west.
—Ed McClanahan, author of *Famous People I Have Known*, and *O the Clear Moment*

Dove Creek is a beautifully wrought novel which tells a tender story of a woman who loved and learned lessons of the heart on the Nez Perce and Coeur d'Alene reservations of northern Idaho.
—Mary Clearman Blew, author of *All But the Waltz and Balsamroot*

WWW.PAULAMARIECOOMER.COM/OTHER-BOOKS-BY-PAULA-MARIE-COOMER/
DOVE-CREEK/

Summer of Government Cheese

Paula Coomer's fine work is characterized by a palpable sense of place as well as by a strong compassion for, indeed love for, her idiosyncratic characters.
—Valerie Miner, author of *After Eden* and *Winter's Edge*

What has charmed me about Paula Coomer's stories evinces itself here in spades: her joyfully comic yet genuinely humane engagement with a fictive bus full of quirky and lovable characters; her meandering narratives that never lose their true course; and the drop-dead gorgeous lyricism that continually possesses her and transforms one's sense of what language is and can do.
—Lance Olsen, author of *Nietzsche's Kisses* and *Anxious Pleasures*

WWW.PAULAMARIECOOMER.COM/OTHER-BOOKS-BY-PAULA-MARIE-COOMER/
SUMMER-OF-GOVERNMENT-CHEESE/

ALSO BY PAULA MARIE COOMER

Blue Moon Vegetarian: Reflections, Recipes, and Advice for a Plant-Based Diet (Memoir/Cookbook) Former nurse Paula Marie Coomer lives life as a vegetarian for a year in order to see its effects on her health. Part memoir, part cookbook, and part health-and-nutrition how-to for becoming and staying a vegetarian.

Dove Creek (Literary Fiction) After a disastrous and abusive marriage, single mother Patricia draws on her Cherokee roots for courage. She finds her place as a Public Health nurse, but she must constantly prove herself—to patients, coworkers, and family members—in her quest to improve the lives of others.

Summer of Government Cheese (Fiction - Short Stories) A collection of darkly introspective short stories. As they say, one way to dispel darkness is to expose it to light.

www.ingramcontent.com/pod-product-compliance
Lightning Source LLC
Chambersburg PA
CBHW051253110526
44588CB00026B/2983